MW01291897

The Writer's Lexicon Volume II

More Descriptions, Overused Words, and Taboos

Kathy Steinemann

Print Edition

ISBN-13: 978-1983583582
ISBN-10: 1983583588

Table of Contents

Foreword

Anne R. Allen

I'm honored to introduce Kathy Steinemann's second volume of *The Writer's Lexicon*. The first book provides such a wealth of information about words and usage that it's a must-have for all writers, from beginners to long-time pros.

I think you'll find this continuation just as valuable.

I grew up loving words. My parents were both Ivy League college professors with PhDs in English Literature and Classics. Debates at the family dinner table were often solved by bringing out our huge two-volume "compact" version of the Oxford English Dictionary (the one with the magnifying glass). My parents felt that disputes often came from miscommunication and misuse of language. So we'd ferret out the roots of a word in order to pin down its precise meaning and understand its nuances and connotations.

Kathy's books help a writer explore those nuances and connotations in order to choose the perfect word for any occasion with precision and creativity.

And you don't need a magnifying glass.

Unlike a standard thesaurus, *The Writer's Lexicon* provides words in context as well as dozens of examples of usage. It also offers alternatives for overused words and phrases as well as edited examples of ways to enliven your writing by choosing exactly the right word.

The Writer's Lexicon is unique in its scope and helpfulness. (It even provides writing prompts to jumpstart your storytelling.) It's a boon to all writers, whether they write fiction or nonfiction.

When she visited our writing blog, Kathy offered a sample from this book in her post "Filter Words and Phrases to Avoid in Writing Fiction." It received 5000 hits per day for five days straight—the biggest five-day readership we have ever had on our multi-award winning blog.

Logophiles and writers, this is a book you'll turn to again and again. Enjoy!

—

Anne R. Allen is an award-winning blogger and the author of twelve books, including the bestselling *Camilla Randall Mysteries*. She's the co-author, with Catherine Ryan Hyde, of *How to be a Writer in the E-Age: A Self-Help Guide*, and has recently published *The Author Blog: Easy Blogging for Busy Authors* with Kotu Beach Press. Anne blogs with *New York Times* million-seller Ruth Harris at *Anne R. Allen's Blog...with Ruth Harris* (annerallen.com), which was named one of the 101 Best Websites for Writers by *Writer's Digest.*

Why I Wrote This Book

Kathy Steinemann

During my writing endeavors I often found myself creating alternatives for overused words. I saved those word lists in a manual on my computer and developed many into blog posts.

Several of my blog followers urged me to publish the lists. I expanded them to produce *The Writer's Lexicon: Descriptions, Overused Words, and Taboos*.

But it didn't end there. Over the following year I created more alternatives. They became the basis for *The Writer's Lexicon Volume II: More Descriptions, Overused Words, and Taboos*.

As you write, realize that dialogue trumps so-called writing "rules." People come from various backgrounds and professions. Readers won't expect a preschooler to use perfect grammar, nor will they tolerate a thug who communicates like a university professor.

When not writing, pay attention to everything and everyone around you. Jot down ideas or dictate them into your cell phone before they escape your busy brain.

Sprinkled throughout these chapters you'll find exercises and examples with ideas for story prompts. Snap 'em up at will, and ...

... write on.

P.S. Near the end of this book you'll find a Master Table of Contents that lists the chapters of both volumes of *The Writer's Lexicon*. You can also download a PDF version of the Master ToC at:

https://kathysteinemann.com/toc.pdf

Writing Rules Examined

"Rules" barrage writers from all sides. This chapter dissects a few rules and presents examples of why they might (or might not) be valid.

Rule 1: Do not use semicolons.

Kurt Vonnegut said in *A Man Without a Country*: "First rule: Do not use semicolons. ... All they do is show you've been to college."

Then he flaunted a semicolon pages later in the same book: "Those of us who had imagination circuits built can look in someone's face and see stories there; to everyone else, a face will just be a face."

He went on to say: "And there, I've just used a semicolon, which at the outset I told you never to use. It is to make a point that I did it. The point is: Rules only take us so far, even good rules."

Maybe the rule should be: *Avoid* semicolons.

Rule 2: Avoid present tense.

Present tense jars readers, and although it can make a story seem more immediate, it works best when contrasting with events that happened in the past.

The Hunger Games Trilogy by Suzanne Collins and *Divergent Series* by Veronica Roth are written in present tense. Although I enjoyed the books, I was reminded on every page that I felt uneasy. In *Allegiant,* the third *Divergent* book, head-hopping and first-person present tense made it difficult at times to remember whose head I was in.

Present tense seems almost a fad nowadays. Will it die the same death as pet rocks?

Rule 3: Avoid adverbs.

Mark Twain's advice: "If you see an adverb, kill it."

Stephen King's opinion: "The adverb is not your friend. ... Adverbs, like the passive voice, seem to have been created with the timid writer in mind."

But the works of both writers include occasional adverbs.

Consider *The Adventures of Tom Sawyer* by Mark Twain:

"Amy chatted <u>happily</u> along ..."

"... and then stepped <u>quickly</u> but <u>cautiously</u> ..."

And *Mile 81* by Stephen King:

"The stone on Carla's chest was <u>suddenly</u> gone."

"... and began to pedal <u>slowly</u> toward the end of Murphy Street."

Conclusion: Adverbs may improve writing if deployed with caution.

Rule 4: Avoid lengthy descriptions of places and events.

Description functions like any other creativity tool. In moderation, it performs well. However, too much detail may engender purple prose and plodding narrative.

Skeptical? Study the following:

Susan stepped into the brightly lit kitchen and tucked a lock of long espresso-brown hair behind one ear. The luscious fragrance of garlic, ground beef, and dill in Alton's homemade tomato spaghetti sauce wafted into her nostrils, evoking a strong memory of its delicious taste. The bubbling sauce spat a hissing red globule onto the glass cooktop of the stove. Her fingers trailed over the smooth surface of the newly remodeled center island. "Mmm, smells good," she murmured as she nibbled on his neck. "By the way, your mom just texted me. She'll be about an hour late."

The paragraph stimulates all five senses—sight, smell, taste, hearing, touch—but is there a reason for so many words? The situation is simple. Susan wants to inform Alton his mom will be an hour late for dinner. He's making spaghetti. Maybe she can catch him before he boils the water for the pasta. She's in a hurry. Reducing the flowery prose will speed the narrative:

Susan hurried into the kitchen. "Mmm. That smells delish," she said, as Alton's bubbling spaghetti sauce spat a hissing globule onto the stove, "but your mom just texted me. She'll be an hour late."

A reduction in words speeds to the crux of the paragraph.

Comprehensive descriptions are critical in fantasy and science fiction. However, a detailed account of a McDonald's restaurant in a modern-era novel? Not so much.

Conclusion: This rule is practical when employed judiciously.

Rule 5: Avoid detailed descriptions of characters.

This dovetails with Rule 4.

Although readers usually don't need to know about every clothing wrinkle or the brand of a person's shoes, they require enough description to form a mental picture. That description should occur when characters are introduced, before readers develop their own ideas of what they look like. Do you want everyone to imagine your six-foot-three blond jock as a medium-height brown-haired man, only to be ambushed by your conflicting description halfway through the story?

Too much description = bloated narrative.

Too little description = confused readers.

Conclusion: Rule 5 is another practical rule if applied wisely.

Rule 6: *Show*, don't *tell*.

Keep Rules 5 and 6 in mind as you scrutinize the following:

Caileen looked at me, like she was an angry panther ready to pounce. Her face turned red, and her chin jutted so far forward I thought she might lose her balance. "Why didn't you tell me you were fired?" she demanded.

Readers will know that Caileen is angry, but all the *show* slows the narrative.

Caileen's angry eyes flashed. "Why didn't you tell me you were fired?"

Caileen's angry eyes represent a classic *tell*. Paired with a strong *show* verb, this paragraph reduces the word count to less than one-third.

Conclusion: *Show, don't tell* works much of the time. However, when you need to speed the narrative or conserve word count, strategic *tells* produce excellent results.

Rule 7: Avoid clichés. Create original expressions.

This advice is beneficial, with limitations. Your original expressions will sound like clichés if you repeat them ad nauseam. Readers might gloss over a simile such as *mad as a wet hen* even if it appears multiple times in a book. However, include a memorable phrase like *mad as a crocodile late for a frog feast* too often, and people will notice it—not in a good way.

Be original, but don't pat yourself on the back and repeat your clever comparisons multiple times per novel.

Rule 8: Avoid anything except *said* to attribute dialogue.

Stephen King advises in *On Writing: A Memoir of the Craft*: "The best form of dialogue attribution is **said,** as in **he said, she said, Bill said, Monica said.**"

Back to his book *Mile 81*:

"A bunch of teenagers had approached the old deserted house, and when one of them saw the door standing ajar, he'd <u>whispered</u>, 'Look, it's open!' to his buddies."

"'Hurry up, Simmons, or we'll go withoutcha!' Normie <u>yelled</u>."

Many sources claim that *said* is an invisible word. But like any word, if it appears too often it irks readers.

Review this passage:

"You're too old for this," James <u>said</u>.

"Too old?" Beatrice <u>said</u>. "What do you mean by that?"

"Well," he <u>said</u>, "you haven't run a marathon in years. All you do is sit around all day and watch TV."

"You jerk," she <u>said</u>, "you have no idea what I do while you're at work."

"Well, tell me then," James <u>said</u>.

Did the repetition of *said* annoy you?

Try this instead.

"You're too old for this," James <u>said</u>.

"Too old?" Beatrice propped her hands on her hips. "What do you mean by that?"

"Well, you haven't run a marathon in years. All you do is sit around all day and watch TV."

Her face turned red. "You jerk, you have no idea what I do while you're at work."

"Well, tell me then."

Instead of dialogue tags, most occurrences of *said* have been eliminated, or replaced by action beats. The interaction between the characters becomes visible and more compelling.

Conclusion: *Said*, like any word, aggravates if overused.

Rule 9: Do not head-hop.

Examine the following passage:

Edwin felt cold. Shivering, he tugged his coat tight and tried to ignore the biting wind. But Aryana felt warm. She loosened her scarf and used it to wipe beads of sweat off her brow.

In the same paragraph, we see the world through both Edwin's and Aryana's perceptions. Although this type of narrative (third-person unlimited omniscient) used to be popular, modern writers are advised to stick with one character and report the experiences of others through that character's eyes.

Let's rewrite to eliminate head-hopping:

Edwin shivered. He tugged his coat tight and tried to ignore the biting wind as he gazed, astounded, at Aryana—who was loosening her scarf. She even used it to wipe beads of sweat off her brow.

The focal character is now clear, the filter word *felt* is gone, and events are reported from Edwin's perspective.

Head-hopping is used successfully by George R. R. Martin in his *Game of Thrones* series. He confines his head-hopping, otherwise known as point-of-view switches, to separate chapters. Each chapter is chronicled from the POV of one character, and readers are never confused.

Frank Herbert head-hops from paragraph to paragraph in *Dune*. Although confusing at first, his approach provides an atmosphere that supports the almost mystical quality of his narrative. Unfortunately, the POV switches become clumsy and confusing in subsequent novels of the series.

Conclusion: Head-hopping is best avoided.

***Avoid* does not mean *eliminate*.**

Writing "rules" are mere guidelines. If you encounter a rule that begins with *never*, *do not*, or *always*, approach it with suspicion. Learn the rules, and decide when you should bend or ignore them.

Remember Vonnegut's excellent advice: "Rules only take us so far, even good rules."

Dialogue Often Ignores the Rules

You've probably heard the pronouncements of writing gurus hundreds of times:

"Use active voice."

"Eradicate adverbs."

"Avoid repetition."

"Get rid of run-on sentences."

"Eliminate jargon and abbreviations."

However, dialogue should sound real. It should motivate readers to finish "just one more chapter." After another. And another.

Which of the following seems most appropriate?

Dr. Williams peered at Ms. Branch. "Whadaya think I'm doin'? Scratchin' my butt? I'm workin' absolutely as fast as I can, you doorknob."

With his clipped words, impolite language, and adverbs, this character speaks more like a stereotypical construction worker than a doctor.

Dr. Williams peered at Ms. Branch. "What do you think I'm doing, ma'am? Procrastinating? I'm working as quickly as I can, I assure you."

This Dr. Williams sounds like a doctor. He's polite. He practices correct grammar. However, he isn't averse to the occasional adverb.

Dr. Williams peered at Ms. Branch. "What do you think I'm doing? I … I … um … twiddling my thumbs? I've been … uh … working on this for twenty-six hours straight."

This exhausted doctor seems annoyed, but his words are too realistic. Readers dislike clumsy pauses in speech. A better version would be:

Dr. Williams peered at Ms. Branch. "What do you think I'm doing? Twiddling my thumbs? I've been working on this for twenty-six hours straight."

Dr. Williams hasn't slept in over a day. Without being inundated by *ums* and ellipses, we can understand his annoyance.

Can you guess the approximate age of the following speaker?

Matt ran toward Jessica. "Everyone was there, and we had an excellent time. Jack even put in an appearance after his Taekwondo class. You should come next time."

Matt is running, so he's unlikely to be a senior citizen. However, nothing in the dialogue gives us a distinct maturity clue, although the language is too adult for most teenagers.

Matt ran toward Jessica. "Everyone was there and we had an awesome time and Jack even showed up after his Taekwondo class. You should come next time, Mom."

A run-on sentence, simpler words, and the addition of *Mom* reveal that this is a young person—in the same number of words as the first snippet.

Matt scampered toward Jessica. "All the kids were there an' we had an awesome time an' Jack even came after Taekwondo an' can you come next time, Mummy?"

Same number of words, but *scampered*, mispronounced *and*s, a mention of *all the kids,* and *Mummy* distinguish this as an even younger child.

Can you identify the protagonists in these examples?

"I prescribed them p.r.n., and she said she took them for two days. They should have palliated her symptoms by now."

This example breaks the rule about eliminating jargon and abbreviations. However, as long as the writer has provided context, readers will understand that the speaker is a doctor, and they will expect medical terminology.

"C'mon, you can do it. Just one more crunch. One more. One more. One more. Good. Now take a breather and we'll tackle one more set of fifty reps."

This fitness trainer repeats *one more* five times—a classic no-no, but it works in dialogue.

"All right, class. Now that the dry ingredients have been sifted, carefully stir in the milk. Carefully. Good. Now pour the batter into the pans. Quickly. The bell will ring any minute."

This home economics teacher uses passive voice and adverbs, but she sounds like a real person.

"I mowed the lawn and trimmed the hedge and watered the garden real good. It was real, real dry. When I come back tomorrow, I'll weed and mulch the flowerbeds. They really need some TLC."

A landscaper repeats his favorite adverb several times and rattles off one run-on sentence. His repetition of *real* and *really* could be a quirk that sets him apart from other characters.

What's wrong with this?

"As you know, Miss Fitch, Mr. Abernathy is away at the teachers' conference in Atlanta and is not available by telephone between 9 a.m. and 6 p.m. except for extreme emergencies. Your situation hardly qualifies as urgent. Abernathy won't return until March 30. You must wait until then to tender your resignation."

The opening words, *as you know*, provide a clue. Miss Fitch is already aware of the information being relayed by the speaker, and readers should be too.

Have you ever watched a television drama where the characters discuss a situation? Do you zone out after a few seconds and forget the details? Readers will do the same for infodumps disguised as dialogue. Include backstory elsewhere—just enough for readers to understand the narrative without drowning in minutiae.

Characters should portray more than mirror images.

Dialogue functions best when speakers exhibit idiosyncrasies.

Without quirks and breaking the so-called rules, characters will function like cardboard figures cut from the same pattern.

Consider the following:

"I don't know, old chap," said Mr. Dixon. "Five teaspoons of sugar in a cup of tea are a bit excessive, don't you think?"

"Not at all," replied Mr. Flaherty. "I always consume five teaspoons of sugar in my tea."

"Well, I am surprised that you haven't developed sugar diabetes after all these years."

"I? Not I, old chap. I exercise regularly and consume an excellent diet with abundant quantities of fiber and nutrients."

"You must spend a small fortune on sugar, sir."

"Not at all. As owner of Flaherty Sugar-Works, I receive as much sugar as I wish, free of charge."

Although you probably followed the thread and deciphered the speakers, it would have been easier if one or both men had speech quirks. For instance:

"I don't know, old chap," said Mr. Dixon. "Five teaspoons of sugar in a cup of tea are a bit excessive, don't you think?"

"Crapola," replied Mr. Flaherty. "I always take five teaspoons."

"Well, I am surprised that you haven't developed sugar diabetes after all these years."

"Me? Ha. I get lotsa exercise. I eat good."

"You must spend a small fortune on sugar, sir."

"Nope. I own Flaherty Sugar-Works. All my sugar's free."

The edited version leaves Mr. Dixon as is but presents a Mr. Flaherty who clips sentences and spouts informal words. Readers will have no problem understanding who says what.

Bend the rules. Flout the rules.

As long as readers understand the narrative, dialogue *should* defy or bend writing rules. Most of us don't speak like grammar pundits. Fiction should embrace that truth and create memorable characters with speech imperfections.

Except ...

... when those memorable characters speak in dialect—inadvisable unless artfully applied.

Scan the following excerpt from *Uncle Tom's Cabin* by Harriet Beecher Stowe.

"Marcies!" said Aunt Chloe; "don't see no marcy in 't! 'tan't right! tan't right it should be so! Mas'r never ought ter left it so that ye could be took for his debts. Ye've arnt him all he gets for ye, twice over. He owed ye yer freedom, and ought ter gin 't to yer years ago. Mebbe he can't help himself now, but I feel it's wrong. Nothing can't beat that ar out o' me. Sich a faithful crittur as ye've been,—and allers sot his business 'fore yer own every way,—and reckoned on him more than yer own wife and chil'en! Them as sells heart's love and heart's blood, to get out thar scrapes, de Lord'll be up to 'em!"

Did you find Aunt Chloe difficult to comprehend? So will readers.

J. K. Rowling's character Hagrid in the *Harry Potter* books spouts dialogue like:

"It's them as should be sorry! I knew yeh weren't gettin' yer letters but I never thought yeh wouldn't even know abou' Hogwarts, fer cryin' out loud! Did yeh never wonder where yer parents learnt it all?"

Yes, it's dialect—but cleverly created so that readers don't falter multiple times per paragraph. When Harry overhears someone who talks this way, readers recognize the speaker at once.

Try it yourself.

Edit the following examples to indicate age and occupation. As you revise, add details that identify the speakers.

Exercise 1

Aldred nuzzled Ina's neck. "I desire you. Now."

His hot breath shot flames of desire into every cell of her body. She moaned. "But I cannot. I am betrothed to another."

"For three years you have bedeviled me with your charm and wit. Why must you succumb to your father's wishes?" He pushed her out to arm's length.

She bit her lip. "He says my destiny is more important than anyone or anything in the entire universe."

"Destiny? Utter nonsense! What must I do to win your affections? Slay a dragon? Fly to the moon?" His eyes drooped, an echo of his slumped shoulders. "I adore you, Ina, more than life, more than jewels or prestige."

"Oh ..." She sobbed. "I know you do, but the Fates have determined my destiny, and I cannot challenge their will."

Suggested solution

Aldred nuzzled Ina's neck. "I want you. Now. Let's just elope."

His hot breath shot flames of desire into every cell of her body. She moaned. "But I cannot. I am betrothed to another, and I must marry him as soon as I come of age."

"For three years you've toyed with me, made my blood boil. Why must you heed your father? He's just a king, just a mortal, just like me." He pushed her out to arm's length.

She bit her lip. "He says my destiny is more important than anyone or anything in the entire universe. And he says it is inappropriate for me to wed a man of low social standing."

"Destiny? Fie! Just what do I have to do to win you over? Kill a dragon, fly to the moon?" His eyes drooped, an echo of his slumped shoulders. "I love you, Ina, more than life, more than anything."

"Oh ..." She sobbed. "I know you do, but the Fates have determined my destiny, and I cannot challenge their will."

Notes: In the initial example, both speakers exhibit perfect grammar and similar speech patterns. In the suggested solution, Ina's dialogue without contractions reflects a woman of breeding from a bygone era. Her suitor, who likes contractions, comma splices, and *just*, is in a lower social echelon. Although specific ages are not provided, we can intuit that Aldred and Ina are probably in their late teens or early twenties.

Exercise 2

"This is the first time I've ever attempted speed dating." Heat spread from Rhonda's chest into the tips of her ears. *Darn. Why must I always blush when I'm nervous?* "What made you try it?"

Joel raised his eyebrows. "The truth is, I saw your photo and couldn't resist. You look a lot like someone I knew."

"Oh. Is that good or bad?"

"Both."

Rhonda waited for a moment, but he didn't clarify. "That's rather vague, don't you think?"

"Well," Joel replied, "she was beautiful—like you—but not very smart."

"Was?"

"Yes, she died."

Suggested solution 1

"This is the first time I've ever attempted speed dating." Heat spread from Rhonda's chest into the tips of her ears. *Darn. Why must I always blush when I'm nervous? It makes my liver spots look like gargantuan warts.* "What made you try it?"

Joel raised his bushy grey eyebrows. "Well, I spied yer picture and couldn't resist 'cause yeh look lots like a gal I knew."

"Oh. Is that good or bad?"

"Both."

Rhonda waited for a moment, but he didn't clarify. "That's rather vague, don't you think?"

"Well," Joel replied, "she was a fine lookin' gal like you but not very bright if yeh know what I mean, a nurse in my old folks' home."

"Was?"

"Yeah, she died."

Notes: Internal monologue counts as dialogue. Rhonda reveals her longevity by thinking about her liver spots. Joel lives in a retirement home. We can surmise that Rhonda probably does too. So, we have two elderly adults involved in a speed-dating encounter. Joel's distinctive speech patterns, including run-on sentences, differentiate him from Rhonda.

Suggested solution 2

"First time I ever tried speed dating." Heat spread from Rhonda's chest into the tips of her ears. *Darn. Why do I always go red when I'm nervous? It makes my zits look like volcanoes.* "What made you try it?"

Joel raised his eyebrows. "I spotted your photo on a poster in science class and couldn't not try, I guess. You look a lot like someone I knew."

"Oh. Is that good or bad?"

"Both, I guess."

Rhonda waited for a moment, but he didn't clarify. "Huh?"

"Well," Joel replied, "she was beautiful … like you—but dumb as a stump."

"Was?"

"Yeah, she moved to a house a few blocks from the college and ditched me for a freshman over there. I guess she likes dudes with their own wheels."

Notes: Once again, Rhonda's internal monologue reveals a clue about her age. The dialogue of both speakers is appropriate for teenagers in a high-school setting. Joel's nervous speech tic, *I guess,* distinguishes him from Rhonda.

Hmm. Why would a high school promote speed dating?

Overused Words and Phrases

The next twenty chapters examine words that creep into your manuscript, multiplying like the rats of Hamelin.

The first volume of *The Writer's Lexicon* showed how to reduce or eliminate troublemakers such as *beautiful, big, clear the throat, little, said, shrug, very, went,* and a host of others.

Volume II continues with *bad, clenched fists, get, itchy, nice, put, use,* et al.

Afraid

Are you *afraid* of losing readers?

One shortcoming that might spur them to abandon your book is excessive repetition. This chapter presents alternatives for *afraid*.

Actions and reactions of POV characters steer the narrative.

Your character of focus might exhibit fearful behaviors such as the following, which are invisible or inconspicuous to others:

Bad taste in the mouth

Blurred vision

Cold extremities

Compulsive swallowing

Confused thoughts

Depression

Distorted time perception

Dizziness

Dry mouth

Exhaustion

Faked bravado

Feigned exasperation or anger

Flashbacks

Flinching

Forced smile

Goosebumps

Hair on neck and arms bristling

Holding the breath

Hypersensitivity of all senses

Inability to speak

Insomnia

Muscle spasms

Nausea

Numb fingers

Pain in chest

Poor memory

Racing pulse

Rash decisions

Restless feet or legs

Shaking knees

Stifled scream

Substance abuse

Sudden cessation of movement

Sweaty palms

Taut shoulders

Thumping heart

Tight leg muscles caused by flight-or-fight response

Tinnitus

Weak or buckling knees

Non-POV characters also provide fear clues.

Most of the following actions, obvious to everyone, allow a writer to weave a tale without worrying about head-hopping:

Adjusting clothing, distractedly or compulsively

Alienation from acquaintances and family

Angling feet away from object of fear

Audible exhalations

Biting on lip(s)

Blanching

Blocking body with hands or fists

Chewing on pen, pencil, fingernails, hair, or lips

Clenched fingers

Clenched mouth

Closed body position, with hands protecting groin

Clutching tightly at personal possessions

Constricted pupils

Covering face with hands, magazine, scarf, etc.

Cowering

Cringing

Crossing the arms

Curling into fetal position

Darting eyes

Distracted dialogue

Fast, shallow breathing

Fidgeting

Flared nostrils

Flushing

Furrowed brow

Gaping mouth

Gazing in all directions to search for danger

Glistening or damp eyes

Grabbing someone for protection or support

Gulping huge mouthfuls of air

Guzzling large quantities of water, beer, etc.

Hair-twirling

Heart attack

Heavy breathing

Hiding behind someone or something

Hugging oneself

Increasing personal space

Jerky movements

Jiggling change or keys in pocket

Licking the lips

Loss of bladder control

Minimal eye contact and staring elsewhere

Nail-biting

Pacing

Panic attack

Positioning an object in the path of danger

Protecting the back with a wall or barrier

Raising eyebrows and wrinkling brow

Rapid blinking

Recoiling

Repetitive behavior

Retreating in opposite direction of danger

Rubbing arms

Scratching

Screaming

Shaking or tapping feet or legs

Shrill voice

Sighing

Slouching or hunching

Squaring shoulders and assuming hostile stance

Squinting

Stepping backward

Stuttering

Sweating

Talking to oneself

Throat clearing

Tiptoeing

Trembling hands, lips, and chin

Tugging on an ear

Tugging on hair

Turning away

Visible pulse in neck

Vomiting

Whimpering or unrestrained weeping

Whispering

White-knuckled grasp of objects

Wide eyes, which might elevate to staring

Wincing

Wringing hands

Show or *tell*?

If you rely on adjectives, you'll probably be *telling*. Keep that in mind as you review the following lists.

Mild fear could be described by the following adjectives:

Agitated, apprehensive, bothered, cautious, concerned, disconcerted, disquieted, disturbed, doubtful, edgy, flustered, fretful, hesitant, ill-at-ease, jumpy, nervous, on edge, perturbed, rattled, tense, timid, timorous, troubled, uneasy, unsettled

Moderate fear requires stronger adjectives:

Alarmed, angst-ridden, anxious, daunted, demoralized, discomposed, dismayed, dispirited, distraught, distressed, frightened, in a tizzy, intimidated, muddled, ruffled, scared, shaken, spooked, unnerved, upset, vexed, worried

Extreme fear demands extreme adjectives:

Aghast, anguished, dazed, dumbfounded, freaked, horrified, horror-struck, hysterical, overwhelmed, panicked, paralyzed, petrified, scared stiff, shocked, sickened, staggered, stunned, stupefied, terrified, tormented, traumatized

Nouns that replace *fear* can inspire innovative phrasing.

Create expressions that rely on synonyms for *fear*. For example:

Fright fluttered in her chest.

Foreboding swelled in his gut.

Horror shot through him.

Caveat: Exercise caution to avoid purple prose.

Mark Twain and H.P. Lovecraft spoke of their characters being *dazed with fright*. Modern writers employ the phrase too, as evidenced by over 2000 *Google* results. Cliché? Maybe. Probably best to coin something more original.

Here are a few nouns to get you started. Select those matching the level of fear appropriate for your characters:

A
Agitation, agony, alarm, anguish, angst, anxiety, apprehension

C
Concern

D
Devastation, dismay, disquiet, distress, dread

F
Foreboding, fright

H
Horror

N
Nervousness, numbness

P
Panic

S
Shock, stress

T
Terror, torment, torture, trepidation

U
Unease, uneasiness

W
Worry

Leverage fear by introducing a phobia.

Adding hurdles for characters to overcome—or not overcome—provides opportunities for subplots. Mild symptoms can be exploited to add humor. An extreme phobia could motivate a character throughout an entire novel.

A few common phobias include:

Acrophobia: fear of heights

This could involve pseudo-anxiety *shown* by a character not wanting to clean the eaves, or terror that prohibits someone from standing on a stepladder or using an escalator.

Agoraphobia: fear of open spaces

Mild agoraphobia could plague a CEO who prefers to work in a cubicle rather than a spacious office. However, this phobia might be so extreme that a different character is afraid to leave home even to retrieve something from the doorstep. The person might ignore the doorbell or keep the curtains closed.

Astraphobia: fear of thunder and lightning

Many pets share this fear, hiding or cowering during a storm. Does your protagonist miss an important meeting because he fears being struck by lightning? Or does he disconnect every electrical device in the house when he hears thunder? Maybe he hides under the bed with his cowering Rottweiler.

Aviophobia: fear of flying

This could present as a mild aversion that causes a protagonist to joke about his condition, or it might elevate to a moderate fear including sweaty palms and nausea, to a phobia so extreme he will only travel via ground transportation.

Claustrophobia: fear of enclosed spaces

A character might dread getting into an elevator, and she might make ill-conceived excuses or self-deprecating remarks while she heads toward the stairs: "You guys don't want to ride the elevator with me. I ran out of deodorant this morning." Perhaps she would avoid fetching something from the basement, or refuse to learn scuba diving.

Cynophobia: fear of dogs

Your character might fear certain breeds, or all dogs. Behavior might include avoidance of specific yards in the neighborhood, refusal to work in an establishment with guard dogs, or heart palpitations when being inspected by sniffer dogs in the airport.

Entomophobia or insectophobia: fear of insects

Similar phobias include apiphobia (fear of bees), arachnophobia (fear of spiders), and myrmecophobia (fear of ants). Some characters might flinch at the sight of an insect: "Mimi, get this thing out of the corner. Now." Others might scream or vomit.

Gargalaphobia: fear of being tickled

What would put a bigger damper on a romantic encounter than a woman whose gargalaphobia causes cringes rather than giggles when she is caressed, or who breaks her boyfriend's jaw when he attempts to brush a stray wisp of hair from her forehead?

Herpetophobia: fear of reptiles or amphibians

Your character might dread going outdoors in a rural district where frogs croak at night, or blanch when a server recommends the frog legs appetizer.

Ophidiophobia: fear of snakes

"You want me to go to the zoo with you? Who do you think I am, Noah?" "Weed the garden? No way—there might be a garter snake hiding in the tomatoes." "Watch a movie with you? Sure. ... *Snakes on a Plane*? You gotta be kidding."

Phobophobia: fear of fear

Franklin D. Roosevelt said "The only thing we have to fear is fear itself" and he added that "unjustified terror ... paralyzes needed efforts." Imagine a protagonist who turns off the news on TV because he's afraid he might experience a panic attack, and whose dread of night terrors prevents sleep.

Social anxiety disorder: fear of social interactions

Mild cases might involve an avoidance of conversation. More pronounced reactions could include refusal to answer the telephone, or avoidance of social media. An extreme phobia might cause a character to order takeout for delivery, push cash under the door when the meal arrives, and then collect the food from the hallway after the delivery person leaves.

Trypanophobia: fear of injections

Have you ever seen a macho man pass out at the sight of a needle? This could develop into delightful humor, as long as it's not overdone.

Angry

Are you a civilized writer?

Sigmund Freud said that civilization began the first time an angry person cast a word instead of a rock. Writers cast words. However, those words don't have to include endless repetitions of *angry*.

A 17th-century proverb provides helpful insight: *Actions speak louder than words.*

Review a few ways your characters could express anger.

They might:

Argue and refuse to listen to other opinions

Attack someone verbally or physically

Ball hands into fists

Bare teeth

Clench jaws

Curse

Explode in strident laughter

Flare nostrils

Frown or scowl

Glare

Gnash the teeth

Lash out at people

Lower eyebrows

Make rude gestures

Narrow the eyes

Point a finger at someone

Poke somebody in the chest

Pound fist(s) on furniture or a wall

Scream or yell

Shake a fist

Speak loudly and/or rapidly

Stand with arms crossed

Stomp

Tense until rigid cord(s) form(s) in the neck

Throw a tantrum

Turn red from collar to roots of hair

Don't rule out clichés.

Many platitudes would be appropriate for dialogue, or you could exploit them as idea fodder. Angry characters might:

Act like a bear with a sore head

Be in a black mood

Bite someone's head off

Blow a fuse/gasket/their top

Come down like a ton of bricks on someone

Demand someone's head on a platter

Eat someone alive

Flip someone off

Flip their lid

Fly off the handle

Get in someone's hair

Get their knickers in a twist

Give someone a piece of their mind

Give someone a tongue lashing

Give someone flak

Give someone the rough edge of their tongue

Go ballistic

Go off the deep end

Go postal

Go through the roof

Harp on someone

Haul someone over the coals

Hit the ceiling

Jump down someone's throat

Lay/light into somebody

Lose it

Pick a bone with someone

Raise their hackles

Rap someone's knuckles

Scream bloody/blue murder

Skin someone alive

Stare daggers at someone

Tear a strip off someone

Vent their spleen

Evaluate a few examples.

<u>Example 1</u>

Nora, with an <u>angry</u> red face, told Brandon he wasn't allowed to go to the rave.

Nora's red face *shows* her anger.

Nora's face turned crimson. She shrieked at Brandon, "You're not allowed to go the rave."

A change from *red* to *crimson* emphasizes Nora's emotion, as does the strong verb *shriek*. Converting narrative to dialogue will engage readers, although many writers would remove the comma after *Brandon* and replace it with a period to create an action beat instead of a dialogue tag.

Let's create a different version:

Nora flipped her lid. Then she flipped Brandon off. "You're not gonna go to the rave."

This would work for a story written by an adolescent narrator.

<u>Example 2</u>

"What do you want?" asked Marla, growing <u>angry</u>.

Does Marla *grow* angry, or is she already angry? Having characters start or begin actions should be saved for more appropriate scenarios.

Marla's nostrils flared. "What do you want?" she demanded.

Marla's flared nostrils *show* her anger. Although I recommend limiting dialogue tags, in this case *demanded* seems more appropriate for anger than its milquetoast cousin *asked*.

Yet another twist:

Marla went ballistic, and her voice shot up fifty octaves. "What do you want?" I saw steam coming out of her ears. Literally.

This is another example of a young narrator. It sounds like a teenager's commentary. Literally.

Terrance walked, <u>angry</u> and scowling, toward the door.

Terrance's scowl *shows* his anger. However, we could make the sentence stronger without increasing word count.

With a scowl, Terrance stomped toward the door.

This contains the same number of words—but a more graphic account of Terrance's mood.

Or we could try:

Terrance stomped toward the door, eyebrows drawn so close they could have passed for a bushy caterpillar. His eyes flashed. "It's two a.m. Whaddaya want?"

Do you have any doubt that Terrance is angry? And why?

<u>Example 4</u>

Walden's <u>angry</u> dog grabbed the mail carrier's leg.

Unless this is written from the dog's point of view, we can't know its emotions.

Walden's pit bull gnashed its teeth and attacked the mail carrier's leg.

Gnashing teeth *show* the dog's state of mind. A specific breed well-known for its aggressive nature adds to the intensity, and *attacked* creates a visual that is superior to *grabbed*.

A longer variation:

The mail guy beelined it outta there like a bat outta Hell when Walden's dog growled—but he weren't fast enough. That there pit bull chawed on the dude's leg like it were a jerky treat. No lie.

This narrator might be younger, and certainly comes across as uneducated. Do you have any doubt about the dog's anger?

Example 5

The two <u>angry</u> men were quarreling, and they didn't notice a mugger coming toward them.

We can assume that if the men are quarreling, they're angry. *Angry* could be omitted, or we could attempt something like:

The two men quarreled, voices so loud they set off security alarms, and they failed to notice a mugger slinking toward them.

Loud quarreling *shows* the emotional state of the men, and *slinking* provides a better visual than *coming*.

Another writer might create something like this:

Slinking through shadows, the mugger crept near. Nearer. His targets— two quarreling men—shoved each other, voices growing louder, oblivious to his approach.

Dun, dun, dun. Tension builds. Readers see the angry men and are pulled into the suspense.

Example 6

Pedro gave the girls an <u>angry</u> look and then walked away.

Let's consider the definition of *glare:* to stare in a very angry way.

You can probably guess what the first edit of this sentence will be.

Pedro glared at the girls and then stalked away.

Two strong verbs reduce the word count and create an evocative scene.

Or we could add body language:

Pedro clenched his jaw, mumbled an obscenity at the girls, and hobbled away.

Pedro's mumbled obscenity *shows* his anger. However, he hobbles away. Maybe the girls did something that caused his limp?

Example 7

The <u>angry</u> crowd scared the police chief.

How can the police chief know that the crowd is angry? He's not in their heads.

The deafening roar of the crowd frightened the police chief.

The second example reports the action from the police chief's POV and *tells* how the crowd makes him feel.

Or we could avoid *tell:*

The roar of the crowd drowned out the police sirens. Rioters tossed rocks. They pressed forward, squeezing nearer to the police chief with every shouted obscenity. His trembling hands fumbled for his stun gun.

This example *shows* the crowd's anger and the police chief's fear.

Explore this list of *angry* alternatives.

Showing anger via body language or actions usually requires more words than *telling.* Too much *show* will slow your story and frustrate readers. If you need to *tell*, try one of these words:

<u>A</u>
Acrid, acrimonious, affronted, aggravated, agitated, annoyed, antagonistic, apoplectic, argumentative

<u>B</u>
Bad-tempered, bellicose, belligerent, beside oneself, bitter, blue in the face, boiling, bothered, bristling, brusque, bugged, burning

<u>C</u>
Cantankerous, caustic, cheesed off, choleric, churlish, confrontational, crabby, cranky, cross, crotchety, crusty, curt

<u>D</u>
Discomfited, displeased, disturbed, dour

<u>E</u>
Embittered, enflamed, enraged, exasperated

F
Fed up, fired up, fit to be tied, flaming, flustered, foaming at the mouth, fractious, frothing at the mouth, frustrated, fuming, furious

G
Galled, grouchy, gruff, grumpy

H
Heated, hopping-mad, horn-mad, hostile, hot, hot and bothered, hot under the collar, hot-tempered, hurt

I
Ill-humored, ill-tempered, impatient, in a flap, in a huff, in a state, in high dudgeon, incensed, indignant, inflamed, infuriated, insulted, irascible, irate, ireful, irritable, irritated

L
Livid, looking for trouble

M
Mad, maddened, morose

N
Nettled

O
Offended, on the rampage, on the warpath, ornery, out for blood, out of sorts, outraged, overwrought

P
Peeved, peevish, peppery, perturbed, petulant, piqued, prickly, provoked, put out

Q
Quarrelsome, querulous

R
Rabid, raging, rancorous, rankled, ranting, ratty, raving, riled, roiled, rude, ruffled

S

Seeing red, seething, shirty, short-fused, short-tempered, smoldering, snappish, snappy, snippy, sore, soreheaded, spoiling for a fight, steamed, steaming, stern, storming, stormy, stroppy, sullen, surly

T

Teed off, testy, tetchy, ticked off, touchy, truculent

U

Unreasonable, up in arms, upset, uptight

V

Venomous, vexed, vitriolic

W

Waspish, worked up, wound up, wrathful, wroth

Bad

Can you imagine *The Good, the Bad and the Ugly* with any other title?

I can't.

However, overuse of *bad* will nettle readers.

Multiple connotations exacerbate repetition.

Bad could refer to any of the following:

1. The opposite of good

2. A description for a wicked character

3. Inferior or malfunctioning equipment

4. Shoddy living conditions

5. Something that is wrong, inaccurate, or faulty

6. Anything that causes sickness, harm, or injury

With so many shades of meaning, it's no wonder *bad* appears so often in creative writing.

Nothing speaks louder than examples.

Compare the following groups of sentences and decide which of each is stronger.

Group 1

"You're a bad boy," Sharon said.

"You're a naughty boy," Sharon said.

Experts admonish parents not to demean children but instead to refer to their *actions* as bad. However, either of the preceding statements might be made by a woman flirting with a man.

It's all about context.

Back to the child, consider writing something like the following instead:

"Why did you eat all the cookies?" Sharon propped her hands on her hips. "I told you we were having supper in fifteen minutes."

Now readers see a specific reason for Sharon's frustration.

Group 2

Every ~~single~~ apple on the tree was <u>bad</u>.

Every ~~single~~ apple on the tree was <u>rotten</u>.

Do I need to comment? *Rotten* is more appropriate. Note the strikeouts of *single*. In these examples, the word is redundant.

Let's provide a reason for the rotten apples:

An unexpected hailstorm pelted the apple orchard, creating abrasions that festered into rotting wounds.

Now readers envision cause followed by consequence.

Group 3

A <u>bad</u> battery sent the drone into a catastrophic spin.

A <u>malfunctioning</u> battery sent the drone into a catastrophic spin.

Although *malfunctioning* works as a direct replacement for *bad*, other words that might provide a more concise picture include *shorted, depleted,* and *corroded.*

Maybe we should provide a few details:

Werner cursed. He had replaced the battery and checked the connections. Why was his spy drone spinning ~~out of control~~ toward the sidewalk?

A curse and a question turn the scenario into a paragraph with just enough information to engage readers. *Out of control* could be removed.

Group 4

The <u>bad</u> air filled Nora's lungs, provoking a huge coughing fit.

The <u>polluted</u> air filled Nora's lungs, provoking a huge coughing fit.

Polluted suits the scenario and provides a touch of alliteration. Additional words pulled from the following list could include *fetid, foul, noxious, putrid,* or *tainted.*

We could incorporate more *show* and less *tell:*

Nora groped through the smog, eyes tearing, coughing more with every labored breath.

The previous sentence provides a dramatic image you don't see in the first two examples.

Group 5

"That's a bad assumption," said the professor.

"That's an incorrect assumption," said the professor.

Would a professor use a vague word in preference to one that is more concise?

Perhaps he'd *show* an emotion such as amusement with body language instead of dialogue:

The professor listened to the student's answer, and belly-laughed, holding on to the back of his chair as though he'd collapse if he let go.

Obviously, the student's answer is so ridiculous that the professor can't contain his mirth, a mirth that borders on disdain.

Group 6

"The rent isn't too bad, so I signed the lease," Brett said.

"The rent isn't too steep, so I signed the lease," Brett said.

This connotation of *bad* refers to a monetary amount. Other words to replace *steep* might be *unreasonable, exorbitant,* or *expensive.*

Here's an alternative approach that includes a bit of tension:

"I can afford the rent increase, honestly, I can," Brett said. However, he avoided eye contact with me. I'm sure he was lying.

The narrator could omit the last sentence, and readers would still intuit Brett's uncertainty.

Brandon had a <u>bad</u> reputation.

Brandon had a <u>criminal</u> reputation.

A single edit *tells* about Brandon's reputation, without increasing word count. If room allows, we could pen something more elaborate:

Brandon sold drugs in the shadows, ever alert to security cameras and police patrols.

The last version *shows* why the narrator has such a low opinion of Brandon.

Group 8

Clint's breath was so <u>bad</u> it filled the entire elevator.

Clint's breath was so <u>rank</u> it filled the entire elevator.

The second sentence is better, but we could *show* why Clint's breath is rank:

Clint's <u>barfy</u> breath filled the ~~entire~~ elevator.

Any number of situations and ingested substances could cause bad breath. Pick one. Then incorporate descriptive words that advance your story.

Group 9

I had a <u>bad</u> dream again last night.

I had a <u>terrible</u> dream again last night.

The second sentence is stronger than the first, but English has a word for bad dream: *nightmare.*

I had a nightmare about Hank again last night.

Now we see something specific that piques the interest of readers. Who is Hank? Why would he cause nightmares?

<u>Group 10</u>

The letter contained <u>bad</u> news.

The letter contained <u>devastating</u> news.

Perhaps we should be more specific:

The letter contained a notice of eviction.

The letter contained an obituary for my sister.

With just a few extra words, we incorporate details that could segue into suspense or tragedy. In the next group, we'll continue the thought of a sister's obituary.

<u>Group 11</u>

I felt <u>bad</u> because I hadn't called my sister for three years.

I felt <u>mean</u> because I hadn't called my sister for three years.

Do *bad* or *mean* appropriately describe the emotion sparked by a broken family relationship?

Why hadn't I called Sis before she died? My eyes filled with tears.

Now we *show* the narrator's emotion and remove the filter word *felt*. Identifying the sister as *Sis* makes the paragraph more poignant.

Note the comparative and superlative forms of *bad*.

Remember, it's *bad, worse, worst* (not *bad, badder, baddest*).

However, a protagonist might say something like "Billy's the baddest boy in these here parts, badder than anyone I ever seen."

The protagonist isn't described, but you probably envisioned an uneducated person, perhaps an old fellow with a toothpick hanging out one corner of his mouth.

Alternatives for *bad:*

These adjectives will help you target the connotation you need in your writing.

A
Abhorrent, abject, abominable, abysmal, adulterated, adverse, alarming, amateurish, amiss, annoying, appalling, atrocious, austere, awful

B
Barbaric, barbarous, barfy, base, beastly, befouled, below-par, bent, blah, blemished, blighted, brutal, bum

C
Calamitous, careless, catastrophic, cheap, cheeky, cheesy, contaminated, contemptible, contrary, corrupt, crappy, criminal, cringeworthy, crippling, critical, crooked, cruddy, cruel, crummy, crushing, cursed

D
Dangerous, dastardly, debauched, decadent, decayed, decaying, decomposed, decomposing, defective, defiant, deficient, degenerate, deleterious, depraved, despicable, deplorable, detestable, detrimental, devastating, diabolical, difficult, dilapidated, dire, disastrous, disagreeable, diseased, disgraceful, disgusting, disheartening, dishonest, dishonorable, dismaying, disobedient, disorderly, displeasing, disruptive, distasteful, distressing, disturbing, dreadful

E
Egregious, errant, erroneous, evil, execrable, exorbitant, expensive

F
False, faulty, felonious, fetid, fiendish, flagitious, flagrant, flea-bitten, fleabag, foul, fruitless

G
Galling, ghastly, godawful, grave, grievous, grim, grody, gross, grungy

H
Harmful, harsh, hateful, heinous, hellish, hideous, hopeless, horrendous, horrible, horrid, horrific, horrifying, hurtful

I
Icky, ignoble, ignominious, ill, immoral, imperfect, impish, improper, inaccurate, inadequate, inappropriate, inclement, incompetent,

incorrect, indecent, ineffective, ineffectual, infected, inept, inexcusable, inexpert, infamous, inferior, infernal, iniquitous, injurious, insubordinate, intolerable

J
Junky

L
Lame, lamentable, lawless, loathsome, lousy, low-quality, lowdown, luckless

M
Maggot-filled, maggoty, malevolent, malfunctioning, malicious, marred, mean, meaningless, mediocre, merciless, mildewed, misbehaved, mischievous, miserable, moldering, moldy, monstrous, murderous, mutinous

N
Nasty, naughty, nauseated, nauseating, nefarious, negligent, no-account, nocuous, noisome, not up to par, not up to scratch, not up to snuff, noxious

O
Obdurate, obnoxious, obscene, obstreperous, odious, off, offensive, ominous, out-of-control, outrageous

P
Paltry, pathetic, perfidious, pejorative, petty, pigheaded, pitiful, pointless, poisonous, polluted, poor, preposterous, putrid, putrefied

R
Rambunctious, ramshackle, rancid, rank, rat-infested, ratty, raunchy, rebellious, repellent, repelling, reprehensible, reprobate, repugnant, repulsive, restive, revolting, riotous, rotten, rowdy, rude, ruinous, ruthless

S
Sassy, scandalous, scarred, scurvy, seamy, second-class, second-rate, seedy, senseless, serious, shabby, shameless, shocking, shoddy, sickening, sinful, sinister, sketchy, slipshod, slummy, somber, sordid, sorry, sour, spiteful, spoiled, squalid, stale, stormy, stressful, subpar, substandard, swinish

T

Tainted, tarnished, tawdry, terrible, the pits, third-rate, tragic, traitorous, traumatic, treacherous, troublesome

U

Unacceptable, uncontrollable, uncooperative, undeserving, undesirable, unethical, unfavorable, unfit, unfortunate, unhealthy, unlucky, unmanageable, unpalatable, unpleasant, unprincipled, unproductive, unreasonable, unruly, unsatisfactory, unsavory, unscrupulous, unsound, unwelcome, unwell, unwholesome, unworthy, upsetting, useless

V

Vexatious, vile, villainous

W

Wayward, wicked, wild, willful, woeful, wormy, worthless, wretched, wrong

Exercises and story prompts:

Can you edit out all instances of *bad* in the following? Pay attention to nuances.

Exercise 1

Ariel felt <u>bad</u> about her latest report card. Three <u>bad</u> grades, four mediocre, and one good. But she was so tired all the time. Worst were mornings, when she felt so <u>bad</u> she wanted to upchuck her breakfast. Maybe it was time to tell Drake the truth.

[Readers will assume Ariel is pregnant. Can you twist this into a dramatic surprise? Maybe she ingested poison because of something in the school's environment. Perhaps she's suffering anxiety attacks about a previous or planned action.]

Exercise 2

A <u>bad</u> smell forced its way into the basement through the single crevice Warren hadn't stuffed with rags. A <u>bad</u> feeling crept up his spine as he searched for something to keep the <u>bad</u> vapors from reaching his nostrils. Would the police arrive in time?

Exercise 3

"Bad water, bad food, and bad mattresses." Chelsea threw a moldy pillow onto the floor. "What else does this bad hotel offer? Free fleas and bedbugs?"

Heat crawled from Eddie's chest into his face and ears. "Well if you hadn't blown all our money at that casino and got us kicked out by that bad-ass bouncer, we might have been able to afford something decent."

[Careful. Dialogue should be realistic.]

Exercise 4

Syd's bad humor permeated every thought, every deed. It affected his work performance. Three customers had accused him of providing bad service.

Humph.

Not his fault the car lot was filled with badly serviced lemons. Not his fault his house had been repossessed because of a bad loan with an exorbitant interest rate. Not his fault his girlfriend's body lay beneath the patio stones, just waiting to be discovered by the new owners.

How could he remove the corpse without being caught?

Exercise 5

Black cats were bad luck, right? Then why did Carole win at least $250 every time she lugged Samba along with her when she purchased lottery tickets?

She cradled her cat in the crook of her right arm, whistling as she dreamed of today's win. Ten tickets. She'd buy ten tickets, and then—

Screeching brakes. A thump.

Carole landed on her back, a bad pain knifing through her shoulders, as Samba ran away.

One bad decision, a bad fall, and here we were, stranded at the bottom of an unscalable cliff. The wind was blowing so bad we couldn't keep warm no matter how often we stoked the fire. We huddled together in the bad winter weather and prayed for the rescue choppers to arrive before it was too late.

Because

Readers may raise their eyebrows if they encounter multiple repetitions of *because* within a short passage. Although finding replacements for a building block of the English language is tricky, it's not impossible.

This chapter contains over two dozen alternatives for *because.*

Does this news item irritate you?

Because of the prevailing political climate, those in office avoid encounters with the press. They say it's because of busy schedules, but their constituents say it's because the politicians don't want to stand up for "what's right."

Can we rewrite to exclude *because*?

With the prevailing political climate, those in office avoid the press. They blame busy schedules, but their constituents disagree, accusing the politicians of not standing up for "what's right."

The succinct version relays the same message in a more engaging manner.

Let's review a statement made by an ecological group.

Because of GMOs (genetically modified organisms), humans may one day find themselves facing extinction. We need to act now, because waiting is not an option, because procrastination puts us and future generations at risk, because soon every crop and every animal species used for food will have been genetically modified. Do you want to tell your children and your grandchildren that you didn't act because you were afraid of the GMO bullies?

Can we lower the word count and strengthen the message like we did in the previous example?

GMOs (genetically modified organisms) may one day cause the extinction of humans. Soon, every crop and animal species used for food will have been genetically modified. Prompt action is crucial; procrastination endangers us and future generations. Do you want to tell your children and grandchildren that your fear of the GMO bullies resulted in apathy rather than action?

Fewer words. More direct message. Engaged readers.

However, some writers might prefer the repetitions in the sentence that begins with *We need to act now.* Like the lyrics of "We're Off to See the Wizard," which repeats *because* multiple times as an intentional literary device, the sentence could function as it stands.

Wilbur faces a smelly dilemma.

Because Wilbur's cologne had offended the noses of all partygoers in the banquet hall, he slipped into the men's bathroom for a quick wash. Truth be told, he looked forward to removing the cologne from his pits, because it burned. He stripped to the waist. Unfortunately, his efforts were thwarted somewhat, because he couldn't find any soap. Because of that, he splashed generous quantities of plain water over his upper body.

When he returned to the banquet hall a few minutes later, he couldn't figure out why everyone was gawking at him—until he looked down and realized it was because his crotch was dripping wet.

Poor Wilbur. Can we tighten the narrative?

Wilbur's cologne had offended the noses of all partygoers in the banquet hall. No problem. *He slipped into the men's bathroom for a quick wash, looking forward to removing the burning cologne from his pits. After stripping to the waist, he couldn't find any soap.* Oh well, plain water is almost as good.

When he returned to the banquet hall a few minutes later, he couldn't figure out why everyone was gawking at him—until he glanced down and realized his crotch was soaked.

Which version do you prefer? Note the addition of two internal-dialogue snippets.

Perhaps a colon, semicolon, em dash, or period would solve the problem.

She had no reason to be disappointed, because he showed up on time.

She had no reason to be disappointed: He showed up on time.

She walked to work because her car was out of gas.

She walked to work; her car was out of gas.

I need to go to the meeting <u>because</u> my boss isn't available.

I need to go to the meeting—my boss isn't available.

He was confused <u>because</u> the test didn't make any sense.

He was confused. The test didn't make any sense.

Direct replacements for *because*:

My preference for replacing *because,* or short phrases including it, is to reword. However, the following suggestions will help if you don't have the time or desire for more extensive edits. Beware: Some alternatives will contribute to word bloat. Others might be best suited for dialogue, awkward narrators, or period fiction.

<u>As</u>
~~Because~~ <u>As</u> the woman had no friends, she walked alone.

<u>As a consequence</u>
Obesity has soared in many countries ~~because~~ <u>as a consequence</u> of poor diet and lack of exercise.

<u>As a result</u>
~~Because~~ <u>As a result</u> of his impudence, the teacher gave him a detention.

<u>As long as</u>
~~Because~~ <u>As long as</u> she studied, she received excellent marks.

<u>As things go</u>
~~Because~~ <u>As things go</u>, if he thinks he can win, he will.

<u>Being that</u>
~~Because~~ <u>Being that</u> he arrived late, he missed the appetizer tray.

<u>By reason</u>
He was found not guilty ~~because~~ <u>by reason</u> of insanity.

<u>By virtue</u>
He received a medal ~~because~~ <u>by virtue</u> of his bravery.

<u>Consequently</u>
She works out every day. ~~Because of that~~ <u>Consequently</u>, she is well-toned and healthy.

Considering
~~Because of~~ <u>Considering</u> the extenuating circumstances, I will forgive his absence.

Due to
~~Because of~~ <u>Due to</u> a tornado warning, everyone evacuated the fairgrounds.

For
He loved her ~~because of~~ <u>for</u> her enthusiasm and loyalty.

For the reason that
The process is tedious, ~~because~~ <u>for the reason that</u> every step must be verified by three people.

For the sake
The government must reduce its spending ~~because~~ <u>for the sake</u> of the economy.

Forasmuch as
The stable boy readied the horse and carriage ~~because~~ <u>forasmuch as</u> the mistress desired to drive into town.
[Archaic; useful for historical novels. *Forasmuch as* also appears in some legal documents.]

Given that
~~Because~~ <u>Given that</u> herbicides were banned, the landscaper had to search for other means of weed control.

In light
~~Because~~ <u>In light</u> of her excellent references, we decided to hire her.

In that
His essay was believable, ~~because~~ <u>in that</u> he supported his arguments with comprehensive data.

Inasmuch as
~~Because~~ <u>Inasmuch as</u> the patient had contracted a contagious infection, visitors were required to wear gowns and masks.

In view
~~Because~~ <u>In view</u> of the overwhelming evidence that pollution causes so many deaths, the government passed a new Clean Air Act.

In view of the fact that
~~Because~~ In view of the fact that nobody RSVPed to the invitations, the organizers cancelled the concert.

Knowing as how
He decided to pack his bags and leave, ~~because~~ knowing as how she didn't want him around anymore.

Now that
We can begin the staff meeting ~~because~~ now that the boss has arrived.

On account
He can't run the marathon ~~because~~ on account of his sprained ankle.

On the grounds that
We are rejecting your story ~~because~~ on the grounds that it doesn't fit with the theme of our publication.

Out
She trembled ~~because~~ out of fear.

Owing to
~~Because of~~ Owing to her poor interpersonal skills, she was demoted.

Owing to the fact that
~~Because~~ Owing to the fact that a violent storm swept over the stadium, the game was cancelled.

Seeing
~~Because of~~ Seeing her anger, he decided to keep his mouth shut.

Seeing that
~~Because~~ Seeing that the woodpecker had hammered on the window every morning for a week, she set up a motion-sensitive alarm to scare it away.

Since
~~Because~~ Since the warp drive was damaged, they stopped for repairs.

So [often requires rewording]
~~Because~~ my tooth ached, I booked a dental appointment.
My tooth ached, so I booked a dental appointment.

Thanks to
~~Because of~~ Thanks to his diligence, the project was completed ahead of schedule.

Therefore
I think; ~~because of that~~ therefore I am.

Through
~~Because of~~ Through union bargaining, the employees received a 5 percent raise.

Exercises to test your *because*-cognition:

Remove most instances of *because* by substitution or rewording.

Exercise 1

Millie knew she'd never pass the biology test, <u>because</u> she hadn't studied enough. But the lack of studying wasn't <u>because</u> of anything she had done. It was <u>because</u> she was exhausted. Every night for two weeks, her sleep had been disturbed <u>because</u> Mr. Clarke's dogs barked. And barked. And barked. *It isn't fair. Why should I fail just <u>because</u> the idiot mutts next door can't keep their yaps shut?*

Suggested solution

Millie knew she'd never pass the biology test—she hadn't studied enough. But the lack of studying wasn't her fault: She was exhausted. Every night for two weeks, Mr. Clarke's dogs had barked. And barked. And barked. *It isn't fair. Why should I fail just because the idiot mutts next door can't keep their yaps shut?*

Notes: Adjustments in punctuation eliminate two instances of *because*. The colon in the edited version could have been changed into a semicolon, with *She* becoming *she*; or two sentences could have been created by replacing the colon with a period. Rewording removes all other repetitions, except for one in Millie's internal monologue. Leaving it in makes her thoughts seem more natural.

Exercise 2

<u>Because</u> of antibiotic abuse, many bacteria have become resistant to even the most powerful drugs. <u>Because</u> of this, pharmaceutical companies have been asked to produce new drugs. However, <u>because</u> of

many factors, including insufficient financial incentives for research and development, the number of new drugs entering the market is inadequate.

Suggested solution

Antibiotic abuse has facilitated significant bacteria resistance to even the most powerful drugs. Health professionals and governments have asked pharmaceutical companies to produce new drugs. However, many factors, including insufficient financial incentives for research and development, have resulted in an inadequate number of new drugs entering the market.

Notes: Edits are straightforward, replacing instances of *because* rather than rewording sentences. Note the reduction in passive voice.

Exercise 3

Len bought the biggest, most expensive TV he could find—one with all the bells and whistles. Because he could afford it. Because he deserved it. But as he was setting it up, he discovered that he couldn't read the instructions because they were written in what looked like Cantonese.

Undaunted by this hiccup, he called the local Chinese restaurant. Unfortunately, he had a problem communicating with the person who answered the phone, because she spoke in broken English with a heavy Cantonese accent. Because he couldn't make her understand what he wanted, he decided to drive to the restaurant, instructions in hand. When he showed her the instructions and explained via a combination of sign language and English, she laughed at him.

"You no understand," she said.

"Exactly. I can't understand the words because they're Cantonese."

"No, no, no, you no understand words because they Japanese and you hold page upside down."

Suggested solution

Len bought the biggest, most expensive TV he could find—one with all the bells and whistles. He could afford it. He deserved it. But as he was setting it up, he discovered he couldn't read the instructions, which were written in what looked like Cantonese.

Undaunted by this hiccup, he called the local Chinese restaurant. Unfortunately, the woman who answered the phone spoke in broken English with a heavy Cantonese accent. She had no idea what he wanted.

So Len drove to the restaurant, ~~instructions in hand~~. When he showed her the instructions and explained via a combination of sign language and English, she laughed at him.

"You no understand," she said.

"Exactly. I can't understand the words <u>because</u> they're Cantonese."

"No, no, no, you no understand words <u>because</u> they Japanese and you hold page upside down."

Notes: Extraneous instances of *because* in the exercise are gone. No need to have Len *decide* to drive to the restaurant. In the solution he drives there—period—without the instructions in hand; steering would be difficult if he's clutching something while trying to navigate. Once again, dialogue remains the same.

Blush

Why do people blush?

Writers should know their characters' motivations. Then, readers should be *shown* the cause of each blush. Occasional flushes, reddening of the cheeks, or flaming faces serve a function. However, overuse of these or any other physiological responses will aggravate readers.

Actions speak louder than blushes.

A blush could be caused by:

Adulation, arousal, embarrassment, fear, insecurity, receiving a compliment, remorse, repressed hatred, shame, shyness

A well-placed gesture or action draws readers into narrative. Here are a few ways to *show* motivation without a single blush.

Adulation
Parted lips
Enlarged pupils
Hanging on every word spoken by subject
Complimenting the subject of adulation

Arousal
Sparkling eyes
Flirtatious dialogue
Running tongue over lips
Heavy breathing, accompanied by racing pulse

Embarrassment
Trembling
Shuffling feet
Biting fingernails
Fidgeting or picking fluff off clothing

Fear
Pacing
Trembling hands
Holding the breath
Accelerated breathing

Insecurity
Slumped posture
Focusing gaze on floor or toes
Fidgeting with jewelry or clothing
Clenching bottom lip between teeth

Receiving a compliment
Speechlessness
Expressing thanks
Verbal denial of self-worthiness
Flattering the person who bestowed the compliment

Remorse
Stuttering
Frequent swallowing
Nausea and/or minimal appetite
Looking away from wronged person

Repressed hatred
Bared teeth
Folded arms
Narrowed eyes
Lips pressed together in a thin line

Shame
Trembling
Stooped shoulders
Minimal eye contact
Biting fingernails or chewing on pen

Shyness
Bowed head
Stammering
Pinched lips
Limp handshake

When is a *blush* not a blush?

A protagonist's face might be red due to fever, sunburn, windburn, allergic reaction, or a response to external temperature. But this redness wouldn't be a true blush. Likewise for a protagonist whose face seethes with red—an appropriate phrase to demonstrate anger.

Analyze motivations as you write or edit. Many blushes may be out of place.

Similes and metaphors stimulate the imagination.

You could compare the color in a person's cheeks or face to one of the following:

Apple, cardinal, carnation, cayenne pepper, chili pepper, Elmo doll, fire, flame, ketchup, ladybug, lobster, poppy, raspberry, rose, stop sign, strawberry, tabasco sauce, tomato, wagon, watermelon

Find more red objects by searching the internet for *things that are red.*

Similes usually incorporate *as* or *like.*

The toddler rushed toward her mother, her chubby cheeks as red as an Elmo doll. "Mummmy, Mummmy, pwease don't go."

When Kristy accused Reynaldo of cheating on her, he pulled at his collar, and his face flared red like the ketchup slathered all over his steak and fries.

Metaphors rely on indirect comparisons.

They compare actions or objects that are not normally considered comparable. For instance:

The fire of passion flamed in Elena's face.

Fire of passion is a *tell* as well as a metaphor—acceptable if Elena is the POV character. However, anyone interacting with her wouldn't know her motivation.

It's unwise to make your POV character blush.

Pretend you're embarrassed. Close your eyes and immerse yourself in the situation before reading the next paragraph.

... ...

Back in the real world again?

If you blush, you might feel heat spread throughout your chest and into the roots of your hair, but you won't see your appearance unless you're looking into the mirror.

Likewise with your POV character.

Let's try a few edits.

Example 1

When Aaron presented Alicia with the Employee of the Month award, she <u>blushed</u>.

Since Aaron is introduced by just his first name, readers might assume that these two characters have a relationship. But why does Alicia blush?

When Aaron presented Alicia with the Employee of the Month award, she <u>remained speechless</u>.

Alicia is probably speechless because she has no foreknowledge of the award. In context, other reasons might prove valid.

Example 2

Marian <u>blushed</u> as she stared at Jeremy's coffee mug. "I'm sorry."

Why is Marian staring at the mug?

Marian <u>didn't reciprocate Jeremy's gaze</u>. "I'm sorry. Give me your mug, and I'll make you another coffee. Milk. No sugar."

The second snippet provides a meaningful description. Marian's dialogue and avoidance of eye contact *show* that she's ashamed, maybe even intimidated. We don't need to stack body language with a blush.

Example 3

Zane ogled Melissa's tanned legs, and she <u>blushed</u>.

Ogled is a strong verb that suggests a lecherous intent. Why would Melissa blush?

Maybe she doesn't like Zane or his attitude:

Zane ogled Melissa's tanned legs. She <u>pressed her lips into a thin white line</u>.

Now, readers will know that Melissa doesn't approve of Zane's attention.

Example 4

Shawn <u>blushed</u> when Carrie touched his elbow.

Perhaps Shawn has a secret crush on Carrie?

When Carrie touched Shawn's elbow, his <u>heart raced</u>.

This approach works if Shawn is the POV character. Blushing could be caused by many emotions. A racing heart, however, is a good indication that Shawn has feelings for Carrie.

Carrie touched Shawn's elbow. He <u>blushed</u>.

Same situation as before, with a slight change in wording, but no clear POV. Let's revisit from Carrie's perspective:

Carrie touched Shawn's elbow. His <u>heavy breathing</u> stirred the tiny hairs on her neck, sending a shiver into every cell of her body.

Carrie's response *shows* she reciprocates Shawn's affection. Her reaction is direct, rather than filtering through a phrase such as *She <u>felt</u> his heavy breathing stirring the tiny hairs on her neck.*

Example 5

Daniel could see Estela <u>blush</u> and <u>fidget with her top button</u>.

Estela's motivation might be clear in context—insecurity, perhaps? However, *could see* filters this sentence through Daniel's sense of sight.

Estela's face <u>glowed red</u>. She <u>fidgeted with her top button</u>.

Daniel's name isn't needed. Since he's the POV character, readers see through his eyes.

Example 6

Bonnie <u>blushed</u> to herself whenever she thought of William's washboard abs.

Yes, some authors sprinkle their writing with phrases like *blushed ~~to herself~~.* The last two words are redundant. Everyone can see a blush, and who else would Bonnie blush to? Since she's the POV character, she can't see herself.

Whenever Bonnie thought of William's washboard abs, the <u>heat of desire rushed into her face</u>.

For variety, this sentence changes word order. Heat rushes into Bonnie's face—a *show*. The words also *tell* about her motivation.

<u>Example 7</u>

Doug <u>blushed scarlet</u> when Ms. Pringle sent him to the principal's office. He was embarrassed because he had been caught peeking into the girls' washroom.

A *blush of embarrassment* might work here, but we're trying to eliminate an overused word. Besides, Doug is the POV character, and it's best not to have him blush, especially when the degree of his blush is depicted as *scarlet*. He can't see his own color.

A different approach:

Doug <u>trembled</u> when Ms. Pringle sent him to the principal's office. Why had he allowed himself to be caught peeking into the girls' washroom?

Doug's trembling *shows* his embarrassment, and the second sentence, posed as a question, plants us in the midst of his internal monologue.

Quick alternatives for the verb *blush*:

Note subtle connotations in the following list. Tear-soaked cheeks might glisten red. Slight embarrassment could pinken the face and neck.

Wherever the word *red* appears, it could be replaced with colors such as:

Apple-red, baby-pink, beet-red, blood-red, candy-red, cherry-red, coral, crimson, cupid-pink, devil-red, flame-red, hydrant-red, kiss-red, mango-pink, peach-pink, pink, scarlet, siren-red, valentine-red

Choose a shade that suits your character's personality and circumstances.

<u>B</u>
Blaze, blaze red, bloom red, blossom with fire, blossom with red, burn red

<u>C</u>
Color with red, crimson

<u>E</u>
Erupt with red, explode in red

<u>F</u>
Flame, flare red, flash red, flood with red, flush

<u>G</u>
Gleam red, glisten red, glow red, go red, go red in the face

<u>P</u>
Pinken

<u>R</u>
Radiate red, redden, rubify

<u>S</u>
Seethe with red, shine red, suffuse with red

<u>T</u>
Tinge with red, turn red, turn rosy, turn ruddy

Your turn.

Can you edit away all the blushes?

<u>Exercise 1</u>

In spite of his efforts to control his emotions, Avery <u>blushed crimson</u> when his name was called by Principal Beck. He shuffled to the front of the auditorium and plodded onto the stage, trying to ignore the catcalls and hisses from other students.

Mr. Beck glared down at him. "This is the second time in three weeks. Do you have anything to say for yourself?"

Avery <u>blushed</u>. "Um ..."

[Uh oh. What has Avery done? We know by the principal's glare that it's a no-no. Can you turn this into humor? Horror? Sci-fi?]

The buzzing stopped. Kyle's gaze darted around the room, and he <u>blushed,</u> hoping no one would discover his secret. At least not until _____.

Exercise 3

Madalyn <u>blushed</u> and turned red from the roots of her hair, to her ears, into her generous cleavage. How could she have let this happen again?

[Can Madalyn see her own blushing? What did she allow to happen? Was it something bad? Good?]

But

The simplest words are often the toughest to replace.

Can you imagine devising alternatives for *a, an,* or *the*?

Fortunately, those words don't stand out. Readers usually slip over them without a second thought.

However, *but*, like many words, isn't invisible when it appears too often. Endless repetitions frustrate readers. Likewise with its most common replacement, *however*.

Imagine two people arguing.

Ron leaned toward Edwina. "<u>But</u> you said you would—"

She pointed her finger at him. "<u>But</u> I changed my mind."

They both stood, glaring at each other, <u>but</u> not budging an inch from their spots on the edge of the swimming pool. A voice floated over the fence, <u>but</u> it was too soft to decipher.

Ron yelled, "Who is it?"

<u>But</u> the voice remained silent.

Edwina propped her hands on her hips <u>but</u> kept glaring at Ron. "It's probably your moth—"

"Not his mother," replied the voice, "<u>but</u> I'll give you three guesses. Then I'll throw you both into the pool if you don't kiss and make up."

Whew, seven appearances of *but* in just over a hundred words. Let's consider an edited version:

Ron leaned toward Edwina. "You said you would—"

She pointed her finger at him. "<u>But</u> I changed my mind."

They both stood, glaring at each other, and not budging an inch from their spots on the edge of the swimming pool. A voice floated over the fence—a voice too soft to decipher.

Ron yelled, "Who is it?"

The voice remained silent.

Edwina propped her hands on her hips, continuing to glare at Ron. "It's probably your moth—"

"Not his mother," replied the voice, "_but_ I'll give you three guesses. Then I'll throw you both into the pool if you don't kiss and make up."

This example illustrates how instances of *but* can be reduced by deletion. Seven occurrences have been trimmed to two—in dialogue, where rules about repetition become less important. Even so, the conversation here comes across better with most of the repetitions removed.

Hmm. Who does that voice belong to, and why are Ron and Edwina arguing?

What's happening to Arnold?

Arnold's lips trembled. Nearly a century had crept by, _but_ he would never forget the day he lost Anna. He tried to calm himself, _but_ anxiety battered his thumping heart, which beat faster every moment. His lungs screamed for air, _but_ nothing could get past the spasms in his throat.

He clutched his chest and reached for his cell phone _but_ couldn't force his fingers to cooperate. He slumped to the floor.

Arnold had always feared death, _but_ as Anna's face floated before his eyes, a wave of warmth and peace enveloped him. "Anna," he said, "where have you been?"

Can we replace all instances of *but*?

Arnold's lips trembled. Nearly a century had crept by. _However,_ he would never forget the day he lost Anna. He tried to calm himself. _Even so,_ anxiety battered his thumping heart, which beat faster every moment. His lungs screamed for air, _yet_ nothing could get past the spasms in his throat.

He clutched his chest and reached for his cell phone, _although_ he couldn't force his fingers to cooperate. He slumped to the floor.

Arnold had always feared death. In spite of that, as Anna's face floated before his eyes, a wave of warmth and peace enveloped him. "Anna," he said, "where have you been?"

Did the edited version unsettle you because your brain wanted to think *but* every time you encountered a substitute? Teaching point: Direct replacements for *but* function best if limited.

Let's try a combination edit that relies on both deletion and replacement:

Arnold's lips trembled. Nearly a century had crept by, yet he would never forget the day he lost Anna. He tried to calm the anxiety battering his thumping heart, which beat faster every moment. His lungs screamed for air—air that couldn't get past the spasms in his throat.

He clutched his chest. Reached for his cell phone with fingers that refused to cooperate. He slumped to the floor.

Arnold had always feared death. Why? A wave of warmth and peace enveloped him as Anna's face floated before his eyes. "Anna," he said, "where have you been?"

One direct replacement for *but* remains. Rewording removes the rest.

Sometimes *but* is the better alternative.

Analyze this statement from a man arguing with a buddy in a truck-stop café:

"He avows that he's 'very, very intelligent.' That being said, his actions contradict his words."

This snippet might suit a news commentator or a political scientist, but not a stereotypical trucker.

How about this instead?

"He says he's 'very, very intelligent,' but actions speak louder than words."

The long-winded *but* replacement is scratched, one verb is replaced, and a cliché is added.

Takeaway: Don't slash every occurrence of any word. Analyze each instance.

Direct replacements for *but:*

Explore rewording before you consult this list. Then, if you opt for alternatives, choose with care. Modern fiction novelists might choose differently than period fiction writers.

A
Albeit, all the same, alternatively, although, anyhow, apart from that, aside from that, at any rate, at the other end of the scale, at the same time, at variance with that, au contraire

B
Bar, barring, barring that, be that as it may, besides, brushing that aside, by contrast

C
Contrariwise, conversely

D
Despite that, discounting that, disregarding that

E
Even if, even so, even supposing that, even with that, except, except that, excepting, excepting that, excluding that

F
For all that, forgetting that

H
Having said that, howbeit, however

I
Ignoring that, in any case, in any event, in consideration of that, in spite of that, in the face of that, inversely

J
Just the same

L
Leaving that behind, letting that pass

M
More to the point

<u>N</u>
Nevertheless, nonetheless, not considering that, not taking that into consideration, notwithstanding

<u>O</u>
On the contrary, on the other hand, on the other side of the coin, other than that, overlooking that

<u>P</u>
Passing over that, paying no attention to that, paying no heed to that, paying that no mind, per contra

<u>R</u>
Regardless

<u>S</u>
Save, skipping over that, still, still and all

<u>T</u>
That being said, that said, then again, though

<u>U</u>
Undeterred by that

<u>V</u>
Vice versa

<u>W</u>
What's more, whereas, with that said, with the exception of, without regard to

<u>Y</u>
Yet

Red-pencil time:

Can you edit away all or most instances of *but* in the following exercises?

<u>Exercise 1</u>

Trevor stamped his feet. "<u>But</u> I don't wanna go, Mummy. And you can't make me can't make me can't make me."

Brittney bit her lip, attempting to contain her anger, <u>but</u> she couldn't prevent the sharpness that edged into her voice. "Yes, I can. You've already missed two days of school, <u>but</u> there's nothing wrong with you."

"<u>But</u> I'm hot and my stomach hurts and my throat is sore. ... And ... and ... I can't find my homework."

"You mean the homework you didn't do because you were too busy playing video games?"

He squeezed out a solitary tear.

<u>But</u> his mom didn't fall for it. Trevor could produce tears better than any Hollywood actor. "Ten minutes. You be ready in ten minutes or you're grounded for ten days. No video games. No TV. No dessert."

<u>Suggested solution</u>

Trevor stamped his feet. "<u>But</u> I don't wanna go, Mummy. And you can't make me can't make me can't make me."

Although Brittney bit her lip in an attempt to contain her anger, she couldn't prevent the sharpness that edged into her voice. "Yes, I can. You've already missed two days of school, and there's nothing wrong with you."

"<u>But</u> I'm hot and my stomach hurts and my throat is sore. ... And ... and ... I can't find my homework."

"You mean the homework you didn't do because you were too busy playing video games?"

He squeezed out a solitary tear.

However, his mom didn't fall for it. Trevor could produce tears better than any Hollywood actor. "Ten minutes. You be ready in ten minutes or you're grounded for ten days. No video games. No TV. No dessert."

Notes: For the sake of realism, Trevor's dialogue is untouched. Brittney's single *but* is replaced by *and. Although* and *however* also make guest appearances.

Louis scanned the heads in the crowd. Everyone <u>but</u> Darlene had shown up for the party. He tried to ignore the disappointment in the pit of his stomach, <u>but</u> it gnawed at him so much that he pulled his phone from his pocket. He stared at the screen. *If I call her, she'll think I'm needy. <u>But</u> if I don't call her, she'll think I don't care.*

He tapped his FAVORITES button, <u>but</u> an incoming call interrupted him before he was able to bring up her number. *Another unknown caller? That's the third in less than ten minutes.* <u>But</u> against his strict policy to ignore telemarketers and strangers, he answered.

A voice crackled in his ear. *"Louis? Is that you? I've been trying to reach you, <u>but</u> your phone keeps going to voicemail."*

"Darlene! Where are you? And why isn't your number showing up?"

"It's a burner. <u>But</u> I can't explain right now. Meet me at my place in ten minutes."

"<u>But</u>—"

"Ten minutes."

The line went dead.

Suggested solution

Louis scanned the heads in the crowd. Everyone except Darlene had shown up for the party. Despite his efforts to ignore the disappointment in the pit of his stomach, it gnawed at him so much that he pulled his phone from his pocket. He stared at the screen. *If I call her, she'll think I'm needy. <u>But</u> if I don't call her, she'll think I don't care.*

He tapped his FAVORITES button—

An incoming call interrupted him before he was able to bring up her number. *Another unknown caller? That's the third in less than ten minutes.* Against his strict policy to ignore telemarketers and strangers, he answered.

A voice crackled in his ear. *"Louis, is that you? I've been trying to reach you, <u>but</u> your phone keeps going to voicemail."*

"Darlene! Where are you? And why isn't your number showing up?"

"It's a burner. I can't explain right now. Meet me at my place in ten minutes."

"But—"

"Ten minutes."

The line went dead.

Notes: *Everyone but Darlene* becomes *everyone except Darlene.* The second sentence is reworded to remove *but.* To preserve a feeling of reality, Louis's internal monologue isn't altered. An em dash and new paragraph *show* the interruption of his attempt to bring up Darlene's number. *But against* is changed to *against.* Darlene's first words are left as is, although to amp the pace, *but* is removed from her second bit of dialogue. Louis's final *but* remains as well.

Clenched Fists

How often do your characters clench their fists?

By definition, a fist is a tightly closed hand with the fingers doubled into the palm. So does *clenching the fists* make sense? No. The hand is the body part that clenches to form a fist.

However, a *Google* search for *"he clenched his fists"* produces more than 116,000 results, and *"she clenched her fists"* yields more than 57,800. Perform the searches yourself (including quotation marks) to confirm.

Writers often abuse the most common replacement.

"He balled his hands into fists" generates 19,500 *Google* results

"She balled her hands into fists" generates 15,700 *Google* results

Why the fuss?

Overreliance on *clenched the fists* and *balled the hands into fists* distracts readers.

Direct substitutions often solve the dependence problem.

Try any of the following, or exploit them as triggers for your own alternatives. Careful. Some of these border on purple prose:

Make a fist.

Dig fingernails into palms.

Form white-knuckled weapons with the hands.

Clamp fingers into white-knuckled vise-grips.

Scrunch fingers into angry cannonballs.

Roll fingers into balls of fury.

Fuse fingers into steely clamps.

Curl mitts into menacing missiles.

Lock paws into pugilistic projectiles.

Maybe you need to dig deeper.

Clenched fists might be a sign of:

Aggression, anger, anguish, annoyance, antagonism, anxiety, defiance, determination, flight-or-fight response, frustration, hostility, irritation, jealousy, pessimism, rage, stress, stubbornness, uncertainty, worry

The following list suggests a few ways to *show* these emotions. If you imagine how each emotion makes you react, you could replace *clenched fists* with your own body language or physical responses.

Aggression
Tight jaw
Flared nostrils
Finger-pointing
Invading someone's personal space

Anger
Stomping
Bared teeth
Pulsing vein(s) in neck
Eyes protruding from sockets

Anguish
Insomnia
Quivering
Tense muscles
Visible sweating

Annoyance
Pacing
Folded arms
Terse dialogue
Protruding cord(s) in neck

Antagonism
Glaring
Shouting
Exaggerated gestures
Staring someone down

Anxiety
Grinding teeth
Tugging on an earlobe
Chewing on fingernails or pen
Fidgeting with clothing or accessories

Defiance
Tossing hair or head
Stuffing hands in pockets
Standing with one hand on hip
Jutting chin toward person being defied

Determination
Rubbing neck
Tapping feet or fingers
Touching face or forehead
Pressing lips into a thin line

Flight-or-fight response
Jutting chin
Tense shoulders
Glancing toward the exit
Locking ankles around a chair

Frustration
Scowling
Shaking the head
Snorting or sneering
Biting the bottom lip

Hostility
Kicking furniture
Forming a tight-lipped smile
Leaning toward someone
Smacking desk or wall with palm

Irritation
Narrowing the eyes
Twitchy movements
Massaging the back of the neck
Interrupting someone else's dialogue

Jealousy
Cursing
Rigid posture
Flinging insults
Flushed cheeks

Pessimism
Wrinkling the nose
Making sarcastic remarks
Curling the upper lip
Walking away during a discussion

Rage
Shoving someone
Cracking the knuckles
Jabbing someone's chest or shoulder
Threatening someone with gestures or a weapon

Stress
Wringing the hands
Reddening of the ears
Rubbing arms or stroking hair
Gazing furtively around the room

Stubbornness
Pouting
Fixed stare
Tight mouth
Crossing legs while seated, and grabbing an ankle to lock it in place

Uncertainty
Tentative gait
Fiddling with hair, beard, or mustache
Shifting weight from one foot to the other
Assuming a scissors stance (legs crossed)

Worry
Slumped posture
Unkempt appearance
Repetitive movements
Overindulgence in coffee, cigarettes, alcohol, or drugs

Let's review a few examples.

<u>Example 1</u>

Antoine looked at Tilly and <u>clenched his fists</u>.

Why does Antoine act this way?

Antoine glared at Tilly and tightened his hands so much that his fingernails bit into his palms.

Now we see antagonism, possibly even rage.

Let's *show* another emotion.

Antoine took a drag on his cigarette, the fourth in less than half an hour, and scrutinized Tilly over the top of his glasses. "You could have called and told me you were stuck on the freeway."

This time Antoine *shows* obvious worry.

<u>Example 2</u>

Suzette <u>clenched her fists</u> as she read the webpage.

Is Suzette frustrated? What did she read that would evoke such a reaction?

Suzette bit her bottom lip as she read the bad book review.

Now we see a reason for her emotion—frustration.

Jealousy might also result in clenched fists:

Suzette cursed as she read the glowing book review for her brother's latest novel.

Nothing like an entrée of sibling rivalry, perhaps seasoned with a sprinkling of gender bias.

<u>Example 3</u>

Roland <u>clenched his fists</u> in anger when Elvira showed up three hours late.

Flash fiction might demand a terse sentence such as this. However, *showing* Roland's anger works better for longer works:

Roland bared his teeth at Elvira. "You're late. Again. Three hours this time."

Guess what? The second example contains the same number of words as the first. See—it *is* possible to *show* without becoming longwinded.

Given the degree of Elvira's lateness, Roland might express rage instead of anger:

Roland shoved Elvira against the wall. "You're late. Again. Three hours this time."

Still the same number of words. Fist bump?

Example 4

The crowd clenched their fists in defiance and shook them above their heads. The mayor frowned.

Although this example provides a strong mental image, *in defiance* is a *tell*. Can we *show* the crowd's defiance? Perhaps the narrator would notice the actions of specific people:

The crowd rumbled—a thunderstorm waiting to explode.

One old codger jutted his chin toward the mayor and blew a raspberry.

A middle-aged woman wearing a threadbare jacket tossed her head. "You're an idiot. Nobody can afford more taxes. You expect us to eat our cats so we can survive?"

The mayor cringed.

Note *cringed*, a strong verb that *shows* the mayor's reaction better than *frowned*.

In this passage, *show* requires many more words than *tell*, but we could relate the events in a way that would please a flash-fiction editor:

The crowd groaned when the mayor announced an increase in taxes. He scanned their angry faces—and cringed.

This version increases the word count by two.

Example 5

In anguish, Lois <u>clenched her fists</u>.

Why is Lois in anguish?

Quivering, Lois stared at her father's grave.

Now we have a reason for Lois's distress, with only one extra word.

Another version might read:

Lois grabbed the telephone before it finished its first ring. It slipped from her sweaty palm and dashed into pieces on the sidewalk. "No, no, no, no, NO! Now the kidnappers have no way to contact me."

More words, but now we have the makings of a suspenseful story.

Your turn.

Can you remove all instances of *clenched fist(s)* from the following?

Exercise 1

Mike's <u>clenched fists</u> hung at his sides, dead weights, immovable no matter how much he willed them to open. An unseen force flung him to the ground. He groaned. "Why are you doing this to me?"

[Seems like Mike is in trouble. Science fiction? Fantasy?]

Exercise 2

Veronique raised one <u>clenched fist</u> in a victory salute as she crossed the finish line.

Petra, two strides behind, <u>clenched her fists</u> in anger. *That little b****. If she hadn't _____, I would have won.*

[Is this an athletic event, or can you twist it into something unexpected?]

Exercise 3

When Brenda Fitzgerald entered the foyer, Gerard <u>clenched his fists</u>. *Self-aggrandizing little priss. That suit must have set her back at least a thousand bucks.* He <u>unclenched his fists</u> and offered his right hand. "And how's my wife's divorce attorney today?"

Brenda sneered. "You mean *ex*-wife."

He snatched an envelope from the shelf above the coat rack. "Not according to this."

She <u>clenched her fists</u>. "How did you find out?"

[You might need a lawyer to help you concoct a twist for this one.]

Get

Meet Herb, a man visiting a farmers' market.

Herb __got__ twenty oranges from Jenny's Fruit Stand.

How did he get the oranges? Note the connotations of the following edits:

Herb __bought__ twenty oranges from Jenny's Fruit Stand.

Herb __pilfered__ twenty oranges from Jenny's Fruit Stand.

Without providing any description of Herb's backstory or appearance, the substitution of one word changes readers' opinions of him.

Evaluate the verbs in the following sentences.

Cecelia __got__ an allowance of $15 per week.

Cecelia __earned__ an allowance of $15 per week.

Cecelia __banked__ an allowance of $15 per week.

The first Cecelia gets an allowance. Period.

The second Cecelia works for her allowance. Her diligence could reflect in other areas of her life. Maybe she excels at school because she studies and takes good notes.

The third Cecelia deposits her allowance in the bank. Is she saving for a car, perhaps?

__Get__, __borrow__, or __commandeer__?

Dean __got__ a car.

Dean __borrowed__ a car.

Dean __commandeered__ a car.

Lackluster Dean gets a car.

A more interesting Dean borrows a car. Perhaps he doesn't own one, or his car is in the shop.

Is the third Dean a detective on someone's tail? A military officer? A crook?

Many idioms and phrases begin with *get*:

Some of the suggested replacements that follow are cliché, but they would suit dialogue and some narrators.

Get a clue: become aware, discover, figure out, grasp, realize, understand

Get a free ride: benefit without contributing, receive something free

Get a glimpse: catch sight of, glance at, glimpse, peek at, see, sight, spy

Get hot under the collar: become angry, fly into a rage, lose one's temper

Get a kick out of: be amused by, enjoy, relish, take great pleasure in

Get a life: do something interesting. [Provide a specific example of the interesting activity rather than parrot this phrase.]

Get a load of: concentrate on, focus on, look at, listen to, pay attention to

Get a move on: accelerate, embark on, go, hasten, hurry, hustle, kick off, move faster, rush, set in motion, set off, start the ball rolling

Get a room: go somewhere private, nix the PDA (public display of affection)

Get a word in: barge in, butt in, comment, interject, interrupt, remark, speak

Get across: bring home, clarify, communicate, convey, impart, make clear, pass on

Get along with: agree with, be compatible with, cooperate with, harmonize with, like, relate well to

Get angry: curse, cuss, flare up, fume, boil, rage, seethe, smolder, swear

Get around: circumvent; solve a problem; coax someone to do something

Get at: access, reach, touch; allude, hint, imply, infer, insinuate, intimate, suggest

Get away: beat a hasty retreat, depart, disappear, escape, exit, flee, leave, make a break for it, sally forth, scarper, vamoose

Get away with: avoid punishment; elude, evade; pull off (a joke or crime)

Get back: recoup, recapture, recover, regain, repossess, rescue, retrieve, salvage

Get better: convalesce, improve, mend, progress, rally, recover, recuperate

Get by: cope, deal with, eke, manage (with difficulty), muddle through, survive

Get caught with one's pants down: make a fool of oneself, feel embarrassed

Get close: advance, approach, border on, creep up to, move toward, near

Get dark: blacken, cloud over, darken, dim, grow dim

Get divorced: break up, divorce, split up

Get down: celebrate, dance, groove, hang loose, let one's hair down, paint the town red, party, revel, whoop it up

Get easier: alleviate, assuage, diminish, ease, improve, lessen, lighten, moderate, reduce

Get free: break free, cut and run, escape, flee, run away, take flight

Get going: depart, disappear, go, exit, hit the road, leave, make tracks, split, take off, withdraw

Get hammered/sloshed/trashed: drink like a fish, drink someone under the table, drink too much, party hearty

Get hands on: acquire, come across, come by, discover, find, locate, obtain, procure

Get home: arrive, reach, reappear, return, turn up

Get into: don, put on, slide into, slip into; enter; develop an interest in

Get it: comprehend, cotton on to, follow, grasp, realize, see, see the point, twig, understand

Get it together: fall into place, improve, mend one's ways, progress, reform, shape up, sort out, work out

Get lost: ignore the GPS, lose one's way, lose one's bearings, take a wrong turn; disappear, go away, vanish

Get married: espouse, join in matrimony, jump the broom, marry, say "I do," tie the knot, wed

Get off on: enjoy or be aroused by _____ (a questionable activity or substance)

Get on: be compatible, gel, like, relate, work well with; board, climb on, embark, mount

Get on someone's nerves: annoy, bother, exasperate, frustrate, infuriate, irritate

Get one's due: deserve, earn, justify, merit, prevail, prove worthy, warrant, win

Get one's teeth into: become actively involved, tackle with enthusiasm

Get out: abandon, buzz off, depart, disappear, evacuate, exit, leave, quit, vacate

Get over: accept, come to terms with, conquer, live through, overcome, recover, surmount, triumph over

Get published: publish a book, make the bestseller list, see one's name in print

Get ready: arrange, brace, coordinate, mobilize, organize, prepare, set up, steel oneself

Get rid of: abandon, cast off, discard, dispose of, dump, eliminate, reject, shed, throw away, thrust aside

Get some sleep/shuteye: catnap, doze, grab forty winks, kip, nap, sleep, snooze

Get someone's number: discover the truth about someone, recognize someone's true intentions or motives

Get the best/better of: beat, conquer, defeat, outclass, outdo, outshine, outwit, trounce, vanquish

Get the drop on: act first, seize the advantage

Get the hang of: become proficient, grasp, learn, master

Get the most out of: capitalize on, exploit, maximize, optimize, take full advantage of

Get through: endure, live through, persevere, prevail, stay alive, survive, weather; breach

Get tired: droop, flag, grow weary, run out of steam, slump, tire, weaken, wear out, wilt

Get to one's feet: hop up, jump up, leave one's seat, rise, stand

Get together: assemble, congregate, meet; connect, hook up, link up, make friends, pair off, take up with

Get under one's skin: annoy, bother, frustrate, irritate, peeve, provoke, rub the wrong way, upset, vex

Get up: arise, ascend, rise, stand; awaken, rouse, stir, wake; leave one's bed

Get with it: contribute, do what is expected, improve, partake, participate, progress, take part; realize, understand

Get worse: decline, degenerate, degrade, depreciate, deteriorate, go downhill, weaken, worsen

Alternatives for *get:*

Rather than function as direct replacements, many of the suggestions in this word list will generate ideas and steer narrative in new directions.

A
Accrue, accumulate, acquire, add to, adopt, agglomerate, aggregate, amass, ambush, annex, apprehend, appropriate, arrogate, assemble, assume, attain

B
Bag, bank, borrow, bring in, build up, burgle, buy

C
Cache, cadge, cage, capture, catch, charter, choose, claim, clear, collar, collect, corral, commandeer, compile, confiscate, co-opt, corner, cull

D
Derive, detect, discover, distrain, draft, draw

E
Earn, embezzle, embrace, engage, ensnare, entangle, entrap, excavate, expropriate

F
Fetch, filch, finagle, find, foreclose

G
Gain, garner, gather, glean, glom onto, grab, gross

H
Harvest, heap, hide away, hijack, hire, hoard, hook, hustle

I
Impound, inherit

L
Land, latch onto, lay claim to, lay hands on, lease, liberate, lift, line one's pockets, loot

M
Marshal, misappropriate, mooch, muster

N
Nab, nail, net, nick

O
Obtain

P
Pen (as in confine, imprison), pick, pick up, piece together, pile up, pilfer, pinch, poach, pocket, preserve, procure, purchase, purloin, put by

R

Rack up, realize, reap, recapture, receive, reclaim, recoup, recover, recuperate, regain, rent, repossess, requisition, rescue, retrieve, round up

S

Salt away, salvage, save, scare up, score, scrounge, secure, seize, sequester, shoplift, shoulder, skim, snaffle, snag, snap up, snare, snatch, sock away, sponge, squirrel away, stash, steal, stockpile, store, swipe

T

Take, take over, take possession, thieve, trap

U

Unearth, usurp

W

Wangle, warehouse, win, withdraw, wrest

Exercises to recalibrate your *get* radar:

Replace most instances of *get, gets, got, getting,* and *gotten* in the following. Remember that sometimes dialogue should break the rules.

Exercise 1

Travis **got** into the driver's seat of his dad's car and pressed the gas pedal. It wouldn't budge. "What the f—"

A glance at the floor revealed that a banana had been shoved under the pedal. He **got** angry as he reached down to **get** the banana. "Danika did this. Who else would try to **get** away with something so childish?" He smirked. "I've **got** her number—she's **got** a crush on me."

Suggested solution 1

Travis slid into the driver's seat of his dad's car and pressed the gas pedal. It wouldn't budge. "What the f—"

A glance at the floor revealed that a banana had been shoved under the pedal. He pressed his lips into a thin white line as he reached down to retrieve the banana. "Must've been Danika. Who else would do something so childish?" He smirked. "I've **got** her number—she has a crush on me."

Notes: Changes are straightforward. The last sentence still contains *got*. All other versions of *get* have been removed, including a change from *she's got* to *she has*, although many writers would prefer *she's got*—a common phrase in dialogue.

Did Danika *try* to get away with something, or did she succeed? *Try to* is redundant, and it slows the dialogue. Removed.

Suggested solution 2

Travis <u>slumped</u> into the driver's seat of his dad's car and <u>rammed</u> the gas pedal. It wouldn't budge. "What the f—"

A <u>glower</u> at the floor revealed that a banana had been <u>concealed</u> under the pedal. He <u>cursed</u> as he reached down to <u>seize</u> the banana. "Must've been Danika. Who else would <u>pull</u> something so childish?" He <u>scowled</u>. "<u>Bloody cow</u> is <u>fixated</u> on me."

Notes: The strong underlined words lend a dark mood to the scenario. This Danika comes across as a stalker rather than a lovesick pursuer.

Exercise 2

Andrea's eyes widened when she <u>got</u> a glimpse of the gift-wrapped box. She had never <u>gotten</u> a present from Onithaele on her birthday before. What had changed all of a sudden? Frebondians lived for thousands of years and usually ignored human celebrations. *He <u>gets</u> it. When I see him again, he'll <u>get</u> his due. Maybe now I'll even agree to <u>get</u> married to him.*

Suggested solution

Andrea's eyes widened when she spied the gift-wrapped box. She had never received a present from Onithaele on her birthday. What had changed? Frebondians lived for thousands of years and usually ignored human celebrations. *He finally understands. When I see him again, I'll hug him till his eyes bug out. Maybe now I'll even agree to marry him.*

Notes: The extraneous words *before* and *all of a sudden* have been removed. Rather than thinking that Onithaele will get his due—a vague thought—Andrea envisions a specific action.

Good

Good day. It's good to see you looking for ways to replace *good* in your writing. I plan to give a good look at the alternatives.

Ugh.

Why do we see this word so often?

Good embraces many meanings, including the following:

1. The opposite of bad

2. Well-behaved

3. Satisfactory or desirable

4. Hospitable, neighborly, or kind

5. Honorable

6. Hale or healthy

7. Adequate for a specific purpose

8. Virtuous or moral

9. Providing pleasure

10. Thorough

English adds a hurdle.

Rather than appending *–er* and *–est* for comparative and superlative forms, we say *good, better,* and *best.*

Let's analyze a few examples.

Example 1

Harry had a good imagination.

Harry had a vivid imagination.

Although the second sentence is stronger, it's a *tell*. Can we *show* Harry's imagination instead?

Harry's eyes glazed as he daydreamed of pizzas dripping with extra cheese, rich chocolate milkshakes, and doughnuts dipped in caramel sauce.

Now we see Harry's thoughts, and we gain insight into his character. Note *glazed*, a verb that meshes with the food motif. Do you envision an overweight protagonist? Or an emaciated captive who hasn't eaten for days? The author's responsibility is to expand on this character, to make readers respond positively or negatively.

Example 2

Roberto was a <u>good</u> carpenter.

Roberto was a <u>skilled</u> carpenter.

Skilled is a more appropriate adjective in this situation. Other words pulled from the list in this chapter could include *accomplished, first-rate*, or *talented*.

Can we drop the adjectives and attempt a different approach?

Once they had witnessed his handiwork, Roberto's clients refused to hire anyone else. Carpentry? No—artistry.

Zero adjectives. Strong nouns and verbs instead.

Example 3

Kyle offered several <u>good</u> suggestions, but his wife ignored them.

Kyle offered several <u>helpful</u> suggestions, but his wife ignored them.

Why is Kyle's wife ignoring his suggestions? Are they truly good? Let's *show* a few particulars:

Kyle yelled at his wife over the din of the malfunctioning dishwasher, "You should use the chef's knife. And the other cutting board. And don't forget the garlic."

Leslie continued chopping green onions, gaze focused on the television blaring in the corner.

These snippets represent Kyle's point of view. He thinks his ideas are good. Leslie might not. Maybe she doesn't hear Kyle, or she could be mad because he's an over-controlling misogynist. The writer must provide appropriate details.

Other scenarios? Perhaps Leslie wears a hearing aid. Maybe she's distracted because the baby is crying.

Example 4

Jennie's Flowers & Gifts sells a <u>good</u> assortment of houseplants.

Jennie's Flowers & Gifts sells a <u>diverse</u> assortment of houseplants.

Can an assortment be bad? In this case, *good* could be deleted or substituted with a more appropriate word, as in the second example. Better yet, let's provide specifics:

Jennie's Flowers & Gifts sells hundreds of houseplants, including ivies, rare orchids, and cacti.

No more lackluster scenario; readers will now visualize the various types of plants sold by the shop.

Example 5

"Roger is a <u>good</u> man," Shannon said.

"Roger is a <u>compassionate</u> man," Shannon said.

Other adjectives to describe Roger might include *altruistic, chivalrous, impeccable,* or *well-mannered*, to mention a few. Each word portrays a different image.

Let's assume he's compassionate.

"Roger listens to my problems, no matter how trivial he might think they are," Shannon said. She stared at her toes. "He never interrupts me when I speak. Then he hugs me—you know, that brotherly hug he has for everyone—and I get these feelings that aren't exactly sisterly."

Will Shannon reveal her feelings to Roger? Maybe he really *is* her long-lost brother.

Example 6

Ruby had a <u>good</u> figure.

Ruby had a <u>wicked</u> figure.

The second sentence moves in the right direction. *Wicked* conveys an impression you wouldn't envision with other alternatives such as *exquisite, lovely,* or *terrific.*

Reliance on the infinitives *to have* and *to be*, as so many of the previous examples demonstrate, often result in wishy-washy writing. Let's *show* Ruby's figure.

Whenever Ruby sashayed into a room, all heads snapped in her direction. Gazes, male and female, would begin at her halo of tarnished-gold hair, plummet to her ample cleavage, and stray to her voluptuous hips. She would open her sultry lips, just enough to reveal frost-white veneers, in a supercilious smirk that complemented her haughty head toss.

The narrator provides an opinionated peek at Ruby's character. Will the thoughts prove true, or does this perhaps reflect the assessment of a jilted lover?

Example 7

Finley chose a room with a <u>good</u> view whenever he traveled.

Finley chose a room with a <u>pleasant</u> view whenever he traveled.

Both of the preceding sentences provide subjective impressions. What one reader deems good or pleasant might be the opposite for someone else. Substituting with adjectives such as *exceptional, magnificent,* or *superior* won't clarify the ambiguity, but concise details will:

Whenever Finley traveled, he chose a top-floor room with a view of the beach.

This *shows* that Finley prefers waterfront accommodations and, with three extra words, provides insight into his personality.

Did you notice the change in sentence structure?

Alternatives for *good:*

You won't always have the room or inclination to *show* instead of *tell*. As with every technique, overuse of *show* will bore readers. When you're creating a scene where brevity is crucial, some of these *good* replacements could prove invaluable.

Instead of categorizing words by nuance, I always alphabetize them. Some of the strongest writing and most innovative ideas stem from mixed meanings.

A
A-1, able, acceptable, accomplished, ace, adept, adequate, admirable, adroit, affable, agreeable, all right, altruistic, amiable, amicable, angelic, appreciable, appropriate, apt, awesome

B
Bang-up, beneficent, benevolent, benign, blameless, blue-chip, blue-ribbon, bounteous, brilliant

C
Capable, charitable, chaste, chivalrous, class, classy, commendable, compassionate, competent, complete, compliant, congenial, considerable, considerate, constant, constructive, convenient, cordial, correct, courteous

D
Dazzling, dear, decent, decorous, deferential, delightful, dependable, desirable, devoted, ducky, dutiful

E
Enjoyable, enticing, esteemed, ethical, excellent, exceptional, exemplary, expedient, expert, exquisite

F
Fab, fabulous, fair, faithful, fantastic, faultless, favorable, felicitous, fine, first-class, first-rate, fit, fitting, friendly

G
Generous, genial, gentle, giving, gracious, grand, great, guileless, guiltless

H

Hale, healthy, helpful, high-minded, honest, honorable, hospitable, humane, humanitarian, hunky-dory

I

Ideal, immaculate, impeccable, incomparable, incorruptible, inculpable, innocent, invaluable, irreproachable

J

Jake, jolly

K

Keen, killer, kind, kindhearted, kindly

L

Laudable, law-abiding, likable, lovely, loyal

M

Magnanimous, magnificent, mannerly, marvelous, masterly, meritorious, moral

N

Neighborly, nice, noble, not bad

O

Obedient, obliging, OK, okay, opportune, outstanding

P

Peachy, peerless, perfect, philanthropic, pleasant, pleasurable, polite, praiseworthy, premium, priceless, prime, principled, prized, proficient, profitable, proper, propitious, pure

Q

Quality

R

Reliable, reputable, respectable, right, righteous, robust

S

Saint-like, saintly, satisfactory, satisfying, scrupulous, seemly, significant, skilled, skillful, smart, smashing, sound, special, spotless, squeaky-clean, staunch, steadfast, sterling, strong, sturdy, suitable, super, superb, superior, superlative, supreme

T
Talented, terrific, thorough, thoughtful, timely, tip-top, tolerant, top-notch, treasured, true, trustworthy, trusty

U
Unblemished, unfailing, unimpeachable, unoffending, unspotted, unsullied, untainted, upright, upstanding

V
Valuable, valued, vigorous, virtuoso, virtuous

W
Well, well-behaved, well-mannered, whiter-than-white, whole, wholesome, wicked, wonderful, worthy

Now it's your turn.

Can you remove all instances of *good* in the following?

Exercise 1

"I have a good mind to report you to the police," Dean said. His voice made me shiver. It hung in the alley, an impending thunderstorm casting unease into the shadows.

The hairs on my arms bristled. "But it wasn't my fault. I got a good tip from this good-looking guy on Maple Street."

"Yeah, Maple, where all the prostitutes and druggies hang out."

"No, Maple, where _____ "

[Insert something funny or horrific. Can you twist this into a sci-fi story?]

Exercise 2

It was no good arguing with my wife. Whenever she went into one of her tirades, she informed me she had a good reason for it. But today when she ranted and raved at me like my witch of a mother used to, I grabbed a good _____. [Does the narrator grab a good (gargantuan, heavy, humongous) book and club his wife over the head? A good ol' tire iron, perhaps? Or does he grab a good hug? Can you move this in an unexpected direction?]

I stared at the sticky substance on my fingers. It had been a <u>good</u> three weeks, and it was still as viscous as the day I invented it. *Dental procedures. Manufacturing. Home repairs.* I could make a <u>good</u> billion out of this. Maybe more.

[Our narrator hasn't thought about weapons applications. Many inventions can be repurposed by the military.]

Exercise 4

Ewan was a <u>good</u> friend. No matter how late at night one of his buddies called, he'd throw on his clothes, pick up the drunk from the bar, and drive the guy home—no questions asked.

Friday, however, turned from <u>good</u> to bad within three minutes. In fact, the media called it "catastrophic."

[Does Ewan finally get tired of his role? Does one of his buddies attack him? Does he disappear? Maybe he shows up at a police precinct, spattered with blood and unable to remember his identity.]

Itchy

Are you frustrated because you can't find synonyms for *itchy?*

You're not alone. *Itchy* is a ticklish word with few close relatives.

Ogden Nash once said that happiness is having a scratch for every itch. However, happiness for a writer might be finding the perfect synonym for *itchy.*

You'll encounter snares during your hunt.

The brain sometimes interprets itchiness as pain and vice versa, because the same chemicals trigger both sensations. Hence terms such as *painful itch*. When we scratch an itch, pain often replaces the tickly tingling in an instant.

To complicate the situation, scratching or rubbing—rather than a response to a true itch—might indicate disbelief, doubt, insecurity, or uncertainty.

Body language provides one solution.

If any of the previously mentioned emotions drives your character, try replacing the itch with appropriate nonverbal responses:

Disbelief
Squinting
Cocking an eyebrow
Narrowing the eyes
Rolling eyes skyward

Doubt
Shrugging
Rubbing an eye
Twitching the nose
Shaking the head

Insecurity
Cupped-palm handshake
Fiddling with clothing, jewelry, or hair
Keeping hands close to face during dialogue
Standing with hands clasped in front of groin area

Uncertainty
Frowning
Fleeting smile
Sitting with crossed ankles
Forceful exhalation through pursed lips

Describe the itch.

Adjectives to describe itchiness could include:

A
Annoying

B
Biting, burning

C
Chronic, constant, crawling, cutaneous

D
Deep, dry

E
Embarrassing, endless, everlasting, excessive, extreme

F
Fierce, fiery, frustrating, furious

I
Incurable, insatiable, intense, intolerable, irresistible, irritating

M
Maddening, merciless, mild, morbid

N
Nagging, nervous, never-ending

P
Painful, peeling, perpetual, persistent, prickly, profound, prurient

R
Raw, relentless, runaway

<u>S</u>
Severe, slight, stinging, strong, subcutaneous, sudden

<u>T</u>
Tantalizing, tingly, tormenting, tortuous

<u>U</u>
Unbearable, unbridled, uncomfortable, uncontrollable, unignorable, unpleasant, unreachable, unrelenting, unscratchable

<u>V</u>
Vague, violent

Invent adjectives.

Lewis Carroll and William Shakespeare coined new words. So can you.

An itch could be goose-bumply, pricklish, tinglish, scritchy, or scratchity.

Put your imagination to work, and then ensure that your context leaves no uncertainty about what the new words mean.

Capitalize on comparisons.

A character could:

Feel like ants/gnats/lice are crawling into every crevice, crack, and pore

Have a neck that itches as though someone is watching

Have a throat that burns and itches like it contains an anthill

Have arms that itch as though they have been clad in a wool sweater for weeks

Have eyes that itch like they haven't seen sleep in days

Have eyes that itch worse than the time the character stayed up all night drinking in a smoke-filled bar

Have skin that itches as though ticks are burrowing into it

Itch as though being tickled by feathers

Itch as though sleeping on a bed of fiberglass

Itch as though stung by nettles

Itch like a fresh scab waiting to be picked off

Itch like a million mites are marching into the nose

Itch like a scar begging to be scratched

Itch worse than the itchiest poison-ivy rash

Show the itchiness.

Have your characters scratch, scrape, scrabble, bite, gnaw, scrub, massage, kneed, or rub the affected body part(s).

Adjectives to replace *itchy:*

As you review these options, remember that only POV characters can relay sensations. If a person is being viewed by someone else, body language and/or dialogue should *show* the itchiness.

B
Bumpy, burning

C
Chafed, chapped, crawling, crawly

F
Flaky, flea-bitten

I
Inflamed, irritated

P
Prickling, prickly

R
Rash-riddled

S
Scratchy

T
Tickly, tingling, tingly

<u>U</u>
Uncomfortable

Scrutinize the following examples.

<u>Example 1</u>

Doris had <u>itchy</u> eyes.

This is an easy one to fix.

Doris rubbed her eyes.

If Doris has allergies, you could make them an integral part of your story, *showing* her sneezing, avoiding animals or allergens, and talking with a nasal tone.

<u>Example 2</u>

Tom was <u>itchy</u> to find a new client.

In this context, *itchy* means *eager, antsy,* or *restless.* A search in your favorite thesaurus would provide alternatives, or you could *show* Tom's motivation:

Tom needed to find a new client before month's end, or he'd lose his productivity bonus.

If a character's circumstances are urgent, *itchy* won't serve as a suitable adjective.

<u>Example 3</u>

Connie squinted at the phone through dry, <u>itchy</u> eyes.

Stacked modifiers are best avoided. The easiest solution would be to remove *itchy* from the example. Or we could *show* the itchy dryness:

Connie squinted at the blurry screen on her phone. She yearned to claw at her dry eyes and quell the burning tickle.

<u>Example 4</u>

Every time Justin entered the public showers without flip-flops, he ended up with <u>itchy</u> athlete's foot.

The easy solution is to remove *itchy*. The majority of readers will know what athlete's foot feels like. Or we could *show* the itchiness:

Every time Justin entered the public showers without flip-flops, he spent the next few days scratching the fungal infection on his feet.

Example 5

Fred hated the itchy collar on his new coat.

Perhaps *itchy* isn't the best adjective in this case. A new coat collar might be better described as *prickly* or *scratchy*. Or we could try another approach:

Fred rubbed at the rash caused by the collar on his new coat.

Example 6

Eight days since Marie had shaved her legs. How could anyone live this way? They were so itchy!

The question is good, but the exclamation point? Not so much. We could emphasize the itchiness in another way:

Eight days since Marie had shaved her legs. How could anyone live this way, scratching at stubble and applying calamine lotion every few hours?

Example 7

The relentless, itchy, biting sensation kept Rob awake all night.

More stacked adjectives, and we don't know what is causing Rob's distress. His blankets? A rash? A new beard? Let's reveal the reason:

Rob woke several times during the night and found his stubby fingers scratching, unbidden, at his scruffy six-day-old beard.

Ready to tackle a few exercises?

Remove all instances of *itch* and *itchy* in the following.

Exercise 1

As Zach stared at his itchy, bumpy face in the mirror, he applied alcohol to the red welts, flinching with each dab. How could he have been so stupid?

[What caused the welts? Mosquitoes? Bedbugs? Spiders? Perhaps something unexpected or imaginative?]

Exercise 2

The ginger cat felt horribly itchy. But he could never resist rolling in catnip, no matter how allergic he was to the sweet-smelling, addictive stuff.

[How can the writer know how the cat feels? POV problem. However, this approach might work for children's books, or fantasy where cats think like humans.]

Exercise 3

Nathan stepped out from behind the curtain and glanced at the audience. Then his gaze was drawn, inexorably, to his exposed skin. Itchy hives glared up at him under the blazing floodlights.

He resisted the urge to scratch, at least for now, and cleared his throat. "O calamine, calamine. Wherefore art thou, calamine?"

[Why does Nathan have hives? Can you turn this into a humorous soliloquy?]

Exercise 4

Maddie twitched her itchy nose. A vase above the fireplace fizzled and transformed into a black cat. She scowled. "Darn, I've done it again."

Although her tortuous itch begged to be scratched, she scooped up the confused feline. "Sorry, Tobias, I have to send you back."

The cat hissed and twitched his tail. "No way you're gonna send me back there." He bounded out of Maddie's arms and into the kitchen faster than she could blink.

[These two characters share previous history. Can you include backstory without boring readers?]

Like Similes

Like similes are *like* ice cream.

You enjoy that first creamy spoonful or imaginative simile. If you ingest too much too quickly though, you suffer brain freeze. No matter how palatable *like* similes are, a bellyful will unsettle readers.

Likewise with similes that incorporate *as*.

Keep in mind the difference between a simile and a metaphor.

Simile: a figure of speech that compares two things. It often includes *like* or *as*. *Eyes like marbles. Yellow as a banana.*

Metaphor: a figure of speech that uses one kind of object or idea in place of another to suggest a likeness. *She was green with envy.*

Many similes can be eliminated by *showing*.

Colleen tossed the heirloom into the trash like a banana peel.

Let's ignore the simile for a moment and analyze the sentence. Without a comma preceding *like*, the trash resembles a banana peel.

Colleen tossed the heirloom into the trash as though it were a banana peel.

Better. But we can remove the comparison and retain the banana-peel reference:

Colleen tossed the heirloom into the trash along with the banana peels.

Now we *show* Colleen's disregard for the heirloom. Without a simile.

A strong-verb punch KOs many similes.

Example 1

Edwin talked like an angry ape.

Apes grunt, gibber, and bellow. They might even roar, screech, or ooh-ooh-ooh. In the spirit of the writer's intent, let's try:

Edwin bellowed.

Bellow means to utter a loud roar in anger or pain. No need for a simile.

<u>Example 2</u>

Carlos treated his three-year-old daughter <u>like</u> a princess.

Like a princess has lost its impact. A *Google* search yields more than 8,000,000 results.

Strong verb to the rescue:

Carlos doted on his daughter.

Dote means to adore, idolize, pamper.

Many authors would prefer to add details:

Carlos doted on his daughter, buying her expensive toys and designer clothing.

<u>Example 3</u>

Josh followed Dyanne, <u>like</u> a bloodhound sniffing after its prey.

Let's rewrite this:

Josh stalked Dyanne, showing up "by accident" at least once a day.

A stronger verb and a specific example provide engaging details.

<u>Example 4</u>

With all its wrinkles, the old man's face looked like tree bark.

A simple remedy:

With all its wrinkles, the old man's face resembled tree bark.

Or we could remove the tree-bark analogy:

A tangled web of deep wrinkles obscured the old man's face.

A tangled web of deep wrinkles evokes a different mental image than tree bark, but both images are compelling.

Ponder the pig, a creature that frequents many similes.

Rewording *shows* the meaning behind each comparison.

Act like a pig

He made lewd propositions to every woman he met.

He picked his nose in public.

Burp like a pig

His rumbling burp overpowered the blaring rock music.

A belch erupted from his maw.

Eat like a pig

He devoured everything in sight and then asked for more.

He shoveled food into his mouth, belching and talking at the same time.

Look like a pig

Food stains covered the front of his shirt, and his pants bulged at the seams.

His jiggling belly flopped over the top of his belt, hiding it under liberal layers of fat.

Pink like a pig

His porky face gleamed, pink and sweaty, in the sunlight streaming through the window.

She chose a putrid piggy-pink for the living-room curtains.

Snort like a pig

She snuffled while she slurped her soup.

Her swinish snort caught me by surprise. I couldn't determine whether she was laughing or choking.

Squeal like a pig

A high-pitched squeal was her only response when she spied the engagement ring.

His porcine squeal of fear echoed from the walls of the canyon.

Stink like a pig

He reeked of body odor and garlic, with a fetid undertone reminiscent of pig feces.

To say the stench of her cooking reminded me of a pig farm would be an insult to the pigs.

Sweat like a pig

His clammy shirt clung to his body, and sweat poured from his brow into his eyes.

She squirted perspiration from every pore, creating a muddy river that coursed down her chest and into her pock-marked cleavage.

Waddle like a pig

He waddled away, butt cheeks waggling in his sloppy jeans.

She shuffled down the sidewalk, in a clumsy, swaying motion. I almost expected to see a curly pig's tail peek out from under her jacket.

More common similes and simple replacements:

Act like a bully: badger, browbeat, bully, harass, intimidate, persecute, terrorize, threaten, torment

Act like a timid horse: balk, cower, cringe, flinch, recoil, retreat, shrink back, shy, spook, start, wince, withdraw

Chatter like a magpie: babble, blabber, blather, burble, gabble, gibber, jabber, natter, prate, prattle, rattle on, yammer

Climb like a monkey: clamber, monkey up, mount, scale, scrabble, scramble, shin up, shinny

Cling like a burr: adhere, affix, attach, bond, cement, clasp, clutch, fuse, glue onto, hold fast, latch onto, stick

Crawl like a snake: creep, glide, meander, slide, slink, slither, snake, sneak, twist, wind, worm, wriggle, writhe

Crawl like a spider: creep, inch, lurk, prowl, scamper, scrabble, scramble, scuttle, sidle, skulk, slither, sneak, spider

Cry like a baby: bawl, blub, blubber, boo-hoo, howl, mewl, pule, shriek, scream, sniffle, snivel, sob, wail, whimper

Draw like a moth to a flame: allure, attract, beguile, captivate, dazzle, ensnare, entice, enthrall, lure, mesmerize, tempt

Drink like a fish: booze, chug, fall off the wagon, gulp, guzzle, hit the bottle, imbibe, knock back, quaff, slurp, swig, swill, tipple

Eat like a bird: nibble, nip, nosh, peck at, pick at, play with, sample, snack, take tiny bites, toy with

Eat like a horse: bolt down, demolish, devour, gobble, gorge, guzzle, ingurgitate, overeat, scarf, shovel in, stuff, wolf down

Explode like a volcano: blow a fuse, blow one's top, blow up, erupt, go ballistic, hit the roof, lose one's temper, vent

Eyebrows like a caterpillar: bristly, bushy, coarse, frowsy, hairy, profuse, shaggy, unkempt, untamed, wild, woolly

Eyes like headlights: alight, burning, flaming, glowing, on fire, luminous, radiant, smoldering; piercing, sharp, shrewd

Feet like flippers: amphibious; EEEE, enormous, humongous, large; flat; broad, splayed, wide; awkward, clumsy

Fight like cats and dogs: battle, brawl, clash, exchange blows, grapple, row, scrap, scuffle, tussle, wrangle, wrestle

Fist like a hammer: crushing, dangerous, formidable, heavy, iron, overpowering, powerful, strong, unyielding, weighty

Fit like a glove: cling, cocoon, cradle, cushion, envelope, fit perfectly, hug every curve, sheathe, snug, swaddle

Fly like an eagle: drift, float, glide, hover, sail, soar, sweep, take wing, wing

Follow like a puppy: chase, hound, hunt, pester, pursue, shadow, sniff after, sniff around, stalk, track, trail after

Giggle like a schoolgirl: chortle, simper, snicker, snigger, tee-hee, titter, twitter

Go over like a lead balloon: disappoint, disenchant, dishearten, disillusion, dismay, dissatisfy, fail, flop, upset

Grow like a weed: balloon, burgeon, flourish, mushroom, shoot up, spread out, thrive

Have eyes like a hawk: catch every detail, miss nothing, notice every aspect, see clearly, spy

Hit like a ton of bricks: confound, daze, dumfound, flabbergast, numb, overwhelm, paralyze, shock, stun, stupefy

Laugh like a hyena: bark, belly-laugh, chortle, convulse with laughter, guffaw, fall down laughing, hoot, laugh hysterically

Leak like a sieve: dribble out, escape, ooze out, percolate through, pour out, pour through, seep, spurt out, trickle through

Lie as still as a log: freeze, hold one's breath, impersonate a statue, remain motionless, stiffen

Like a bear with a sore head: angry, choleric, enraged, fuming, furious, incensed, infuriated, livid, outraged

Like a rock (1): dense, durable, firm, indestructible, inflexible, resilient, rigid, rugged, solid, stiff, tough, unyielding

Like a rock (2): consistent, dependable, levelheaded, reliable, sound, stable, steadfast, trustworthy, unfailing, unswerving

Like taking candy from a baby: easy, effortless, painless, simple, straightforward, trouble-free, uncomplicated

Look like a drowned rat: brush sodden hair out of the eyes, drip buckets, leave a damp trail wherever one walks, squish while walking

Look like a penguin: don a tuxedo; wear a black suit and white shirt; flap about; shuffle, strut, waddle; preen, primp

Look like two peas in a pod: bear a pronounced resemblance, echo, harmonize, match, mirror, parallel; share identical ideologies

Move like a snail: crawl, creep, edge, glide, inch, sidle, slide, slither, worm; chillax, dawdle, idle, laze, loll, lounge, postpone, procrastinate

Neck like a pipe: angular, bony, emaciated, fragile, gaunt, pipe-thin, rickety, scrawny, skeletal, skinny, spindly, unstable

Roar like a dragon: bellow, blare, blast, boom, gnarl, resound, reverberate, rumble, snarl, thunder

Run like a cheetah: arrow, barrel, bolt, dash, fly, hurtle, pelt, race, rocket, speed, sprint, tear, whizz, zip, zoom

Run like a frightened rabbit: bolt, break away, cut and run, escape, flee, hare, hop and run, take flight, zig-zag

Scream like a schoolgirl: caterwaul, howl, keen, screech, shriek, shrill, squall, squawk, squeal, wail, yelp, yowl

Sing like an angel: cantillate, carol, chime, chorus, croon, harmonize, serenade, trill, warble

Sit like a bump on a log: dawdle, diddle, dog it, doze, goof off, idle, laze, loaf, loll, lollygag, malinger, shirk

Sleep like a log: conk out, crash, cuddle up with Sleeping Beauty, die for eight hours, emulate Rip Van Winkle, saw logs, snore, zonk out

Smell like a rose: appear innocent, seem respectable; carry off, cope, manage, overcome, pull off, succeed; smell sweet

Smell like garbage: give off putrid fumes, offend the nose, pong, reek, smell rotten, smell foul, stink, stink to high heaven

Sound like fingernails on a blackboard: grate, grind, rasp, screech, scratch, scritch, shrill

Stick out like a sore thumb: contradict, contrast, differ, diverge; bulge, distend, jut out, mismatch, project, protrude

Sting like a bee: bite, burn, jab, pound, prick, prickle, punch, smart, spear, stab, throb, tingle, wound

Swim like a fish: cruise, fin, float, glide through the water, pollywog, sail, scud, skim, wiggle

Taste like ambrosia: delight the palate, seduce the tongue, titillate the taste buds

Taste like crap: cause one to gag, end up in the garbage, turn "food" into a four-letter word, leave a nasty aftertaste

Twinkle like stars: flicker, glitter, shimmer, sparkle, wink

Walk like a duck: dodder, flatfoot-it, hobble, meander, pad, shamble, shuffle, toddle, totter, waddle, wiggle, zig-zag

Walk like an elephant: clomp, clunk, galumph, lead-foot, lumber, plod, pound, stomp, stump, thump, thunder, tramp

Work like a dog: graft, grind, drudge, grapple, hustle, labor, moil, slave, slog, strain, struggle, sweat, toil, travail, wrestle

Your turn.

Examine something you've written, and select half a dozen *like* similes. If you can't find any, pat yourself on the back. Otherwise, proceed to the next paragraph.

Are the similes cliché? Do a *Google* search. If you find more than a hundred results matching each phrase, the answer is yes. Can you harness stronger verbs or adjectives? Rewrite as unique metaphors? Or create distinctive *like* similes?

Nice

Nice is ~~a nice~~ an unpretentious word that doesn't pack a lot of punch.

Closely related to *good*, it embraces numerous connotations, including:

1. Pleasant or delightful

2. Congenial or kind

3. Requiring precision or accuracy

4. Subtle or fine

5. Refined or cultured

Nice can be complimentary or derogatory, depending on context:

"That's nice." Jerome smiled and patted Kate on the shoulder.

"That's nice." Jerome sneered and gave Kate the finger.

How many instances of *nice* can you find in your WIP?

Disregard dialogue. Speech should sound realistic. However, the rest of your text will resonate better with readers if you remove *nice* wherever possible.

Let's explore a few examples and analyze how we could revise them.

Example 1

It's nice to be appreciated by my students.

It's heartwarming to be appreciated by my students.

Heartwarming sets an uplifting mood. However, both sentences provide generalizations—*tells* that could be made stronger by *showing:*

Whenever my students smile at me as they grasp a new concept, I tell myself that my humongous debt for eight years at university was worth every nickel.

Teaching fills me with joy, especially when my students get that expression, that look of understanding. I can almost hear them shout "aha" in their heads.

The suggested edits paint word pictures with specifics that don't shout "backstory."

Example 2

Aaron was a nice guy.

Aaron was a sociable guy.

Although *sociable* suggests more than *nice*, it could represent either a positive or a negative impression. Let's consider a couple of ways we could *show* more about Aaron:

Aaron socialized with every chick on the street, ignoring me while he laughed and flirted.

Aaron always stopped to talk with the homeless people on the street.

Two Aarons: one not so nice, the other compassionate.

Example 3

The scarf looked nice against Sofia's cheeks.

The scarf looked becoming against Sofia's cheeks.

Why does the scarf look nice or becoming? Can we create more compelling sentences?

The blue of the silk scarf complemented the blush in Sofia's cheeks.

The muted reds of the chenille scarf matched Sofia's rosy cheeks.

Now, readers will envision color and texture. The more senses we involve, the more striking the descriptions.

Example 4

The city contains several nice parks and playgrounds.

The city contains several peaceful parks and playgrounds.

Peaceful presents a better description, but a writer could substitute other adjectives:

The city boasts several <u>lush</u> parks and playgrounds.

The city is blessed with several <u>large</u> parks and playgrounds.

Lush and *large* provide different impressions that could segue into more details.

Example 5

It was a <u>nice</u> day.

It was a <u>pleasant</u> day.

Pleasant to a skier could mean sunny and cold after a night of snow. A surfer might welcome a windy day, but a snorkeler would prefer calm conditions:

Marie gazed up the slope as she waited in line for the T-bar. Sunlight streamed through the treetops, glistening on the fresh snow. She inhaled the crisp air, and smiled.

Marie gazed at the ocean. Wavelets rippled toward shore, reflecting sunlight that sparkled like tiny gems among the brilliant blues and greens. She inhaled the scent of seaweed, and grinned as she pulled on her snorkeling fins.

The appeal of the day is *shown* in both paragraphs without resorting to synonyms for *nice*.

Example 6

The apple tasted <u>nice</u>.

The apple tasted <u>wonderful</u>.

Why would a person enjoy an apple?

Melanie bit into the apple and chewed slowly, inhaling its aroma and savoring every delectable crunch.

The fragrance and delicious sweetness of the McIntosh apple reminded Melanie of Mom's fresh-baked apple-crisp pies.

The edited sentences embrace multiple senses. Is your mouth watering?

<u>Example 7</u>

Renko always smelled <u>nice</u>.

Renko always smelled <u>marvelous</u>.

Does Renko smoke a pipe? Perhaps he wears a pheromone-based aftershave. Maybe he works in a candy shop:

Renko's aftershave wafted through the room, a delicate musk that promised sensual delights to any woman who succumbed to his charms.

The aroma of licorice permeated Renko's clothing, his hair, his breath. Salivating women flocked around him, like children hoping for treats on Halloween.

Specifics create intriguing situations that engage readers.

<u>Example 8</u>

Nat and Omar had a <u>nice</u> chat.

Nat and Omar had a <u>sociable</u> chat.

The impact of these sentences would prove stronger if we had some idea of Nat and Omar's relationship. They could be estranged brothers, enemies, or business associates, for instance:

Nat and Omar ordered their bodyguards to holster their guns. Then the two men sat and sipped tequila while they discussed their differences.

Tension adds intrigue and substance. Rather than guzzle tequila, Nat and Omar sip. This *shows* a level of distrust. Neither man wants his senses dulled by too much liquor.

Nat and Omar haggled over the price of the Elvis album, neither willing to budge, but smiling as they bartered.

Here we see two people engaged in good-natured negotiations.

Instant alternatives for *nice:*

For those occasions when you require direct replacements, evaluate these adjectives. Many will serve as seeds, sending your imagination in new directions.

A
Accessible, admirable, affable, agreeable, amenable, amiable, amusing, appealing, approachable, attractive

B
Becoming, befitting, benevolent

C
Caring, charismatic, charming, cheerful, commendable, compassionate, congenial, considerate, convivial, copacetic, cordial, courteous, cultured, cute

D
Dandy, delicate, delightful, disarming, discerning, distinguished, divine, ducky

E
Easygoing, enchanting, engaging, enjoyable, entertaining, entrancing, exact

F
Fair, fantastic, fascinating, fastidious, favorable, fine, fine and dandy, friendly, fussy

G
Genial, genteel, gentle, gentlemanly, good-humored, gracious, gratifying, great, gregarious

H
Heartwarming, helpful, honest, honorable, humble

I
Ideal, interesting

J
Jovial

<u>K</u>
Kind

<u>L</u>
Ladylike, likable, lovely

<u>M</u>
Mannerly, marvelous, methodical, meticulous, minute

<u>O</u>
Obliging, open-hearted, open-minded

<u>P</u>
Painstaking, peaceful, peachy, personable, pleasant, pleasing, pleasurable, polished, polite, precise, prepossessing, proper, punctilious

<u>R</u>
Refined, rigorous

<u>S</u>
Satisfying, seemly, simpatico, sociable, solicitous, sophisticated, subtle, swell, sympathetic

<u>T</u>
Tender, thoughtful, tidy, trim

<u>U</u>
Unassuming, unpresumptuous, unpretentious, unselfish, upright

<u>V</u>
Virtuous

<u>W</u>
Warmhearted, welcoming, well-bred, well-mannered, winning, winsome, wonderful

Exercises and story prompts:

Eliminate all or most instances of *nice* in the following.

<u>Exercise 1</u>

After tossing his gun into a garbage bin, Koby took a <u>nice</u> stroll around the block. Shoulders hunched, he entered a <u>nice</u> little bistro on Market

Street and sat with his back to the wall at a <u>nice</u> table in the corner farthest from the street.

He ordered a <u>nice</u> lunch, his gaze never straying from the door.

[Would a description or brand name for the gun make the situation more realistic? If this turns into science fiction, the gun could be a blaster or a laser pistol. An inventive name for the street and bistro could add humor or intrigue.]

Exercise 2

"<u>Nice</u> to meet you," Uber-General Kenald mumbled as he extended one of his twelve tentacles toward Donric.

Donric gaped at Kenald's mottled green skin, and his gaze slowly took in the immensity of the Bathiriian representative. *Nice? Humph. I'll show him <u>nice</u>.* He inclined his upper body in a <u>nice</u> bow—well-rehearsed and exactly as he had been taught by his Bathiriian diplomacy tutor. "My pleasure, Uber-General."

Kenald's upper scent glands hissed a huge puff of foul fumes. "How dare you insult me in such insolent fashion." A tentacle darted from a warty orifice and whipped across Donric's face.

[Donric obviously has a pre-conceived hate toward the Uber-General. Why? And how did he insult the Bathiriian? Can you turn this into humor?]

Exercise 3

Witch Saradon was <u>nice</u> to her three young visitors. She served them <u>nice</u> servings of apple pie topped with dollops of whipped cream. The desserts were followed by <u>nice</u> heaps of jellybeans and chocolates. When the children were ready for a <u>nice</u> snooze, the old witch showed them to a bedroom with <u>nice</u> pillows and toys.

The children woke with <u>nice</u> headaches, in a windowless cell. The only exit? A door constructed of cold metal bars at least one inch thick.

[This could be the setup for a fairy tale or perhaps a nightmare. Even for a fairy tale, though, the language comes across as excessively childish.]

Knut paced around the massive oak coffee table in the living room. *It would be so _nice_ to have at least one day without a call from my mother-in-law, and—Damn!* He snatched the phone from his pocket, scowled at the caller ID, and answered in his _nicest_ voice. "Hello, Knut speaking."

"I know who it is, you good-for-nothing Swede. Who else would pick up your phone? Santa Claus?"

The cords in Knut's neck hardened. "Ho, ho, ho," he replied with his _nicest_ Santa impersonation. "You haven't been _nice_, and you're not getting any gifts this Christmas."

"Well, I never!"

"Yes, you did. At least once. My wife is living proof."

A strangled choke was the only reply. The choke turned into a cough.

And then silence.

"Mrs. Matheson?" Knut stopped mid-stride. "Mother?" He stared at his phone to ensure they were still connected. "Mom?"

[Does Knut's mother-in-law reply? Has she had a heart attack? Or is she stringing him along on a guilt trip? Can you add an unexpected twist?]

Pout

People often pout while flirting or taking selfies. They believe that a pout is sexier than a smile. Your characters might pout when they're upset or unhappy. A pout could accompany other emotions as well.

The most common replacement chosen by writers is *pursed lips*. Unfortunately, the alternate phrase is overused as often as *pout*.

Please don't think you'll fool readers with phrases such as *put on a pout*. No matter how you disguise it, you'll still be branded a repeat pout offender.

Analyze motivations.

A pout could be caused by:

Agitation, aggravation, confusion, contemplation, disapproval, disbelief, dislike, exasperation, flirtatiousness, impatience, irritability, nervousness, pessimism, resentment, sadness, skepticism, suspicion, wariness, worry

Harness body language to *show* these emotions:

Agitation
Fidgeting
Forced laughter
Biting the fingernails
Fiddling with hair or clothing

Aggravation
Sneering
Intimidating glare
Pronounced frown or scowl
Shoving someone's shoulder

Confusion
Stuttering
Cocking the head
Crinkling the nose
Rubbing the chin

Contemplation
Narrowing the eyes
Rocking on heels
Puckering the forehead
Stroking chin with one hand

Disapproval
Squinting
Curling the upper lip
Crossing arms
Tucking tongue into cheek

Disbelief
Mumbling
Scratching the neck
Hesitating before speaking
Spouting disparaging remarks

Dislike
Glowering
Setting jaw and thrusting it forward
Pressing lips into a thin line
Poking someone's chest with an index finger

Exasperation
Flinging insults
Hurried dialogue
Baring the teeth
Making erratic movements

Flirtatiousness
Tossing hair
Preening or grooming
Batting the eyelashes
Running tongue over the lips

Impatience
Standing akimbo
Tapping a foot
Arching eyebrows
Drumming fingers

Irritability
Raised voice
Strained smile
Flared nostrils
Drawing eyebrows together

Nervousness
Perspiring
Dilated pupils
Breathing rapidly
Flinching at sudden sounds

Pessimism
Smirking
Negative dialogue
Derisive laughter
Waving a dismissive hand

Resentment
Rigid posture
Stomping out of the room
Muttering under the breath
Rude or argumentative dialogue

Sadness
Damp eyes
Reticent dialogue
Drooping posture
Stuffing hands in pockets

Skepticism
Biting the lips
Narrowing the eyes
Making derogatory remarks
Smiling in a condescending manner

Suspicion
Eavesdropping
Grinding teeth
Pointing a finger
Accusatory dialogue

Wariness
Adjusting clothing
Tugging on an ear
Excessive swallowing
Tracking a target with the eyes

Worry
Pacing
Grinding teeth
Clenching fists
Adjusting clothing

Five examples of *pout* replacements:

Example 1

A single strong verb can strengthen narrative:

Nicoletta *pouted.* *"But you said you'd be home early tonight."*

Nicoletta *bristled.* *"But you said you'd be home early tonight."*

The second sentence is stronger, but we could make Nicoletta's irritation more intense:

Nicoletta's nostrils flared as she screeched in a tone that could curdle milk, "But you said you'd be home early tonight."

Too much?

A strained smile twisted Nicoletta's lips. "But you said you'd be home early tonight."

Twisted suggests an insincere smile.

Example 2

Do you overplay body language?

Trent pouted and crossed his arms. Then he tucked his tongue into his cheek.

Trent disapproves of something, but the above excerpt contains three action beats. Dialogue could enliven the passage and decrease the number of beats:

Trent crossed his arms. "Do you intend to go out looking like that?"

A minor change, with fewer words, adds conflict.

Example 3

Does your character's pout send mixed signals?

Blaine pouted and nodded simultaneously.

This sentence introduces a conflicted Blaine. We could *show* that in dialogue without the pout:

"I don't know. It seems like a stretch, but I suppose I could go along with it," Blaine said.

Another approach could produce the same effect:

"Sure, whatever you say," Blaine mumbled.

The mumbled dialogue, even though Blaine agrees, *shows* he's unhappy about complying.

Example 4

Do you over-describe?

Cedric pouted, and his lower lip protruded like a big ol' ugly largemouth bass chompin' on a tadpole.

The second part of the sentence provides a memorable description of Cedric's lips. Why use *pout* at all?

Cedric's lower lip protruded like a big ol' ugly largemouth bass chompin' on a tadpole.

The revised version omits redundant details, thereby reducing word count and transporting readers to the rest of the narrative without delay.

Example 5

A well-placed pout may enhance a scene:

Sofie sashayed into the den, wearing nothing but siren-red lipstick and a sensual pout. Jens gasped.

We've set the stage. What happens next? I'd want to know.

Instant alternatives for *pout:*

Try these short substitutions when you don't have the room or desire to *show.*

<u>A</u>
Agonize

<u>B</u>
Bat the eyes, blanch, blench, bristle, brood

<u>C</u>
Carp, chafe, complain, coquet, cringe

<u>D</u>
Disapprove, don a petulant air, dread

<u>F</u>
Flinch, flirt, fret, fume, fuss

<u>G</u>
Grimace, gripe, grizzle, grow petulant, grumble

<u>L</u>
Look petulant

<u>M</u>
Make a cat-butt face, make a long face, make a moue, make a wry face, make eyes at, mop, mope

<u>N</u>
Needle, nudge

<u>P</u>
Pine, pooh-pooh, pother, purse the lips

<u>Q</u>
Quail

<u>R</u>
Recoil

S
Scorn, show displeasure, smolder, snivel, spurn, squawk, squirm, stew, stick out the lower lip, stress, stress out, sulk

T
Tease, thrust out the lower lip, tsk-tsk

W
Wax petulant, wince, wink, worry

Exercises and story prompts:

Remove *pout, pouts, pouted,* and *pursed lips* in the following exercises. As you edit, determine character motivations. Knowing why someone pouts will help you select the best alternatives.

Exercise 1

Manuela's pout transformed her face into a morose mask. I'm sure she intended to mimic a supermodel, but her attempt failed. Dismally.

I ran my fingers over her pursed lips. "Who do you expect to attract with that pout? A lovesick camel?"

She slapped me. Me—the guy who stood by her for at least a billion pouts and three boob jobs. The guy who paid for those boobs. "How dare you!" she said. Her pout disappeared, only to be replaced by a sly smile.

Uh oh. Not again.

[What happened in the past to make the narrator think this? Maybe some of the pouts are necessary. Could Manuela's lips be plumped and pouty because of silicone injections?]

Exercise 2

Mikey pouted. "But I don't wanna go."

His mother pushed him toward the cell door. "It's time."

[Whoa! A child in a cell? Where are these two characters?]

Exercise 3

Leland's face screwed into a <u>pout</u> tighter than a hangman's noose. He glared at the cop. "No way. The light was green when I went through. What kind of racket are you running here?"

Constable Frye's eyes narrowed. "Hands on the wheel, sonny. That's right. Now keep them paws where I can see 'em, and step outta the car, real slow."

Leland's <u>pursed lips</u> relaxed. "Aw, c'mon. My girlfriend will kill me if I miss another _____."

[Another wedding rehearsal? Lamaze class? Donuts Anonymous meeting? Have fun with this one.]

Put

Put-put-put ... What's that? An old jalopy?

Can't be. The spelling is wrong. However, too many occurrences of *put* in your writing might make readers envision a rust bucket.

Put is a weak verb. A writer can often replace it with a single word that *shows* distinct action.

Evaluate a few examples.

Example 1

Nina <u>put</u> her keys on the table.

Not much of a mental picture, is it?

Nina <u>arranged</u> her keys on the table.

This Nina might betray a compulsive need for neatness.

Nina <u>slammed</u> her keys on the table.

Or she could be angry.

Example 2

The cat <u>put</u> one paw in the air and begged for tuna.

Besides the alliteration provided by *put* and *paw*, this sentence provides nothing remarkable.

The cat poked one paw in the air and begged for tuna.

Poked produces a more effective impact than *put*.

The cat raised one paw and begged for tuna.

A stronger verb, *raised*, eliminates the need for *in the air*.

Example 3

Susan <u>put</u> on her makeup.

We could choose a replacement that would decrease the word count by one:

Susan applied her makeup.

A light coat of makeup? A heavy one?

Susan slathered on her makeup.

Another well-chosen verb, *slathered*, provides a strong mental image.

Example 4

Ward <u>put</u> his new painting on the wall.

A slight change enlivens the sentence with sound, while preserving the word count:

Ward nailed his new painting on the wall.

Perhaps Ward is proud of his new painting:

Ward displayed his new painting on the wall.

Three sentences, three verbs, three different scenes in readers' minds.

It's not always that straightforward.

Put appears in numerous phrases. The good news is that single words can replace many of those phrases.

<u>Put a cap on:</u> limit

<u>Put a cork/sock in it:</u> hush

<u>Put a crimp in:</u> disrupt, interfere

<u>Put a damper on:</u> deter

<u>Put a lid on:</u> terminate

<u>Put a plug in:</u> endorse, plug

Put a price on: evaluate, price

Put a spin on: distort, spin

Put a spotlight on: emphasize, highlight

Put a stop to: stop

Put a strain on: overload, strain

Put about: disseminate, inform, spread

Put across: articulate

Put an end to: stop

Put an idea across: persuade

Put aside: allocate, earmark, reserve

Put at risk: endanger, imperil, jeopardize

Put at someone's disposal: lend, offer

Put away: eat; save

Put back together: reassemble

Put back: defer; drink; reimburse; return

Put balls on: masculinize

Put behind bars: imprison

Put behind: forget

Put by: save

Put dibs on: claim

Put down in black and white: pen, record, type, write

Put down roots: settle, stay

Put down: disparage; euthanize

Put food on the table: provide, support

Put forth: propose

Put forward: suggest

Put hair on the chest: energize; toughen

Put heads together: confer

Put in a good word: vouch

Put in a nutshell: abridge, condense, summarize

Put in an appearance: appear

Put in an awkward position: corner; unsettle

Put in for: apply, request

Put in jeopardy: endanger, jeopardize

Put in mothballs: stow

Put in motion: activate, begin, initiate, trigger

Put in one's two cents: comment

Put in place: inaugurate; position

Put in: contribute

Put into action/effect/force: implement

Put into law: enact

Put into practice: do, practice

Put into words: verbalize

Put it mildly: understate

Put money on: bet, wager

Put money up: fund, sponsor, underwrite

Put no stock in: disbelieve, distrust

Put off the scent: distract, sidetrack

Put off: displease; postpone

Put on a pedestal: idolize

Put on airs: gloat, pontificate, swagger

Put on an act: pretend

Put on display: display

Put on ice/hold: postpone

Put on notice: announce; warn

Put on one's thinking cap: reflect

Put on paper: pen, print, scribble, type, write

Put on the back burner: delay, postpone, stall

Put on the griddle: censure

Put on the line: risk

Put on the map: publicize

Put on the nosebag: eat

Put on the Ritz: flaunt

Put on the spot: embarrass, shame

Put on: deceive; don, wear

Put one over on: deceive, trick

Put one's back into it: strain, strive

Put one's butt on the line: risk

Put one's cards on the table: disclose, reveal

Put one's ducks in a row: organize, prepare

Put one's finger on: identify

Put one's foot down: insist

Put one's foot in it: blunder

Put one's foot in one's mouth: blurt

Put one's hand to the plough: work

Put one's heart into: strive

Put one's house in order: organize

Put one's John Hancock on: endorse, sign

Put one's life on the line: imperil, risk

Put one's mind to: concentrate

Put one's name in the hat: volunteer

Put one's nose to the grindstone: toil

Put one's nose where it's not wanted: meddle, pry, snoop

Put one's oar in: interfere

Put oneself in somebody else's shoes: empathize

Put out feelers: investigate

Put out of mind: forget

Put out of misery: euthanize

Put out of sight: hide

Put out the red carpet/welcome mat: welcome

Put out there: propose

Put out to pasture: retire

Put out to sea: sail

Put out: annoy; extinguish; produce, publish

Put over the knee: punish, spank

Put over the top: accomplish, reach

Put plainly: assert

Put pressure on: intimidate

Put right: rectify

Put someone in his/her place: chasten, humiliate, rebuke

Put someone's mind to rest: reassure

Put someone's nose out of joint: irritate, upset

Put something on the street: air, publicize

Put something under a microscope: scrutinize

Put stock/store in: trust

Put sweet lines on: coax

Put teeth on edge: irritate

Put the acid on: beg

Put the arm/heat/screws on: pressure

Put the blame on: blame

Put the brakes on: brake, impede

Put the chill on: ignore

Put the clamps on: block, restrain

Put the clock back: restore

Put the damper on: discourage

Put the fear of God into: intimidate

Put the feet up: relax, sit

Put the genie back in the bottle: revert

Put the hammer down: accelerate

Put the heat/screws/hammer on: pressure

Put the kibosh on: veto

Put the make/moves on: proposition

Put the pedal to the metal: speed

Put through paces: audition, test

Put through the wringer: traumatize

Put to bed with a shovel: bury

Put to bed: conclude, end, finish

Put to death: execute

Put to one side: separate

Put to rest: dispel

Put to shame: disgrace

Put to sleep: euthanize

Put to the sword: slay

Put to the test: evaluate

Put to use: use

Put to work: employ

Put together: join

Put two and two together: conclude

Put under: sedate

Put up: accommodate; erect; can, preserve; finance, fund

Put up a fight: fight

Put up for sale: sell

Put up the shutters: lock

Put up walls: isolate

<u>Put up with:</u> abide, allow, stand, stomach, tolerate

Many more phrases require multiple-word replacements.

I couldn't think of a single verb that would replace *put one's pants on one leg at a time*. Likewise for *put all one's eggs in one basket*. A *Google* search provided the following alternatives.

Put one's pants on one leg at a time: to be an ordinary person; to be a mere mortal.
(http://en.wiktionary.org/)

Put all one's eggs in one basket: make everything dependent on only one thing; place all one's resources in one place, account, etc.
(http://idioms.thefreedictionary.com/)

You'll find hundreds, perhaps thousands, of English phrases that incorporate *put*. Rely on your favorite thesaurus, dictionary, or search engine to locate their meanings. When you find replacements, avoid clichés—except for dialogue, where anything that suits your characters will ring true with readers.

Verbs to replace *put:*

If you need to replace *put* with a single verb, you might find what you need in this list.

<u>A</u>
Abandoned, affixed, anchored, applied, arranged, arrayed

<u>B</u>
Banged

<u>C</u>
Chucked, crammed, crashed

<u>D</u>
Deposited, deserted, discarded, displayed, ditched, dropped, dumped

<u>E</u>
Exhibited

<u>F</u>
Flicked, flipped, flung, forced

G
Glued, grouped

H
Hauled, heaved, hoisted, hung, hurled

I
Inserted, installed

L
Laid, left, lobbed, located

N
Nailed

O
Organized

P
Parked, pegged, pitched, placed, planted, plastered, plonked, plunked, poked, positioned

R
Raised, rested, rolled

S
Set, sited, situated, slammed, slathered, smashed, spread, stabbed, stationed, stood, stuck

T
Tacked, taped, threaded, threw, thumped, tossed, tucked

W
Wedged, winched

Really + Verb Phrases

This chapter examines ways to replace *really* when it appears with a verb.

However, *really* is not the only offender. Beware of qualifiers such as *especially, exceedingly, genuinely, immensely, thoroughly, truly,* and *very.*

Really plays a part in word-bloat.

Many verbs such as the following may not need modifiers. Review each incidence.

~~Really~~ achieve
You will ~~really~~ achieve your goals if you work hard.

~~Really~~ are
The new measures ~~really~~ are beneficial for the economy.

~~Really~~ can
He ~~really~~ can help with the yardwork when he gets home.

~~Really~~ convince
The latest statistics ~~really~~ convince me that global warming is a concern.

~~Really~~ do
What do nurses ~~really~~ do?

~~Really~~ give up
I ~~really~~ give up dieting whenever I see ice cream.

~~Really~~ happen
What would ~~really~~ happen if they fired the missile?

~~Really~~ ignore
Should we ~~really~~ ignore what the scientists say about climate change?

~~Really~~ learn
A hands-on approach is the best way to ~~really~~ learn computer programming.

Really make
How much money can you ~~really~~ make with affiliate marketing?

Really unite
The peace accord will ~~really~~ unite the opposing factions.

Really will
They ~~really~~ will clean up the beach when the weather clears.

Really + verb cheat sheet:

Similar to the previous section, many occurrences of *really* in the following list could just be removed. If emphasis is important, investigate a strong verb or phrase to replace the *really* + verb construction.

<u>Really accomplish:</u> complete, consummate, excel, shine, succeed

<u>Really agree:</u> concur, endorse, formalize, ratify, support, verify

<u>Really allow:</u> approve, authorize, empower, license, sanction

<u>Really annoy:</u> exasperate, frustrate, incense, infuriate, provoke, vex

<u>Really appreciate:</u> apprize, cherish, prize, treasure, value

<u>Really argue:</u> battle, brawl, clash, feud, fight, row, scrap, wrangle

<u>Really ask:</u> beg, beseech, entreat, implore, petition, plead, solicit

<u>Really avoid:</u> abstain, circumvent, eschew, shun, skirt, spurn

<u>Really believe:</u> bank on, count on, depend on, expect, trust

<u>Really belong:</u> befit, click, do, fit, match, measure up, serve, suit

<u>Really bite/chew:</u> gnaw, gore, grind, mangle, maul, mutilate, tear at

<u>Really blame:</u> accuse, censure, denounce, reproach, upbraid

<u>Really blow (1):</u> blast, bluster, burst, gust, rage, storm, surge, whoosh

<u>Really blow (2):</u> disgust, nauseate, repel, repulse, suck

<u>Really blush:</u> burn red, erupt in red, flame, flush, redden

Really bounce: boomerang, carom, jounce, rebound, ricochet

Really brag: crow, gloat, posture, show off, strut, swank, swagger

Really break: crumble, disintegrate, shatter, smash, splinter

Really change: convert, metamorphose, revolutionize, transform

Really check: examine, explore, investigate, probe, scrutinize, study

Really coax: blandish, cajole, inveigle, sweet-talk, wheedle, whine

Really consider: cogitate, contemplate, deliberate, mull over, reflect

Really cry: bawl, bleat, blubber, howl, squall, wail, weep, yowl

Really cut: gash, gouge, lacerate, rip, shred, slash, tear, wound

Really decide: choose, determine, elect, resolve, settle on, undertake

Really diminish: die out, dwindle, fade, melt, peter out, shrink, taper

Really doubt: disbelieve, discount, distrust, question, suspect

Really emphasize: feature, highlight, showcase, stress, underscore

Really enjoy: bask in, delight in, luxuriate in, relish, revel in, savor

Really ensure: assure, certify, guarantee, promise, vouch

Really envy: be jealous of, begrudge, grudge, resent

Really excite: elate, electrify, exhilarate, overexcite, overstimulate

Really expect: await, believe, know, presume, take for granted

Really experience: encounter, face, live through, undergo, weather

Really explain: clarify, elucidate, expound, illustrate, spell out

Really feel: empathize, encounter, endure, experience, suffer, sustain

Really fear: dread, despair, quail at/before, shrink from, worry about

Really fill: cram, load, heap, overfill, pack, stuff, wad, wedge

Really frighten: alarm, horrify, panic, petrify, shock, terrify

Really get (1): accumulate, build up, glom onto, hustle, nail, wangle

Really get (2): appreciate, comprehend, grasp, master, understand

Really grieve: bemoan, bewail, keen, lament, languish, mourn

Really gulp (1): gasp, huff, hyperventilate, pant, puff, wheeze

Really gulp (2): belt down, chug, guzzle, knock back, scoff, swig

Really hate: abhor, despise, detest, execrate, loathe, reject, spurn

Really help: alleviate, empower, enable, encourage, expedite, relieve

Really hesitate: dither, falter, stall, vacillate, waffle, waver

Really hit: pummel, punch, slug, thrash, thump, wallop, whack

Really hold: clasp, clench, cling, clutch, crush, grasp, squeeze

Really hope: anticipate, dream of, expect, look forward to, yearn

Really hurt: ache, burn, pain, pound, rack, sting, throb, twinge, wrack

Really impress: amaze, astound, astonish, dumbfound, shock

Really jump (1): convulse, jerk, recoil, spasm, spring back, start

Really jump (2): bound, hurdle, leap, leapfrog, spring, vault

Really kill: butcher, decimate, destroy, massacre, slaughter, wipe out

Really know: comprehend, conceive, realize, savvy, understand

Really laugh: crack up, guffaw, hoot, snort, split one's sides, whoop

Really learn: absorb, conquer, digest, get the hang of, grasp, master

Really like: adore, idolize, lionize, love, revere, venerate, worship

Really listen: cock the ears, concentrate, eavesdrop, focus, heed, pay attention, prick up the ears

Really look: dig into, focus on, peruse, pore over, probe, rake

Really marvel: admire, gaze in awe, goggle, ooh and aah, wonder

Really matter: carry weight, have an effect, influence, make a difference

Really mean: aver, affirm, avow, declare, insist, maintain, profess

Really miss: ache for, crave, hunger for, long for, pine for

Really need: go without, lack, require, suffer deprivation, want for

Really offend: affront, appall, gall, harrow, mortify, outrage, wound

Really overdo: exhaust oneself, overexert, overextend, work too hard

Really pay: benefit, prove lucrative, reward, yield excellent results

Really please: delight, gratify, inspire, intoxicate, satisfy, thrill

Really pull: heave, jerk, snatch, tweak, wrench, wrest, yank

Really regret: bemoan, deplore, lament, repent, rue, suffer remorse

Really relate: bond, click, connect, hit it off, see eye to eye

Really reveal: advertise, announce, broadcast, foghorn, publicize

Really run: dash, fly, gallop, race, rocket, speed, sprint, zip, zoom

Really seem: echo, embody, epitomize, imitate, mimic, pass for

Really shine: flare, gleam, glint, glisten, shimmer, sparkle

Really shiver: judder, quake, tremble, vibrate

Really show: demonstrate, display, exhibit, flaunt, lay bare, parade

Really smile: beam, flash the teeth, grin, radiate happiness

Really startle: alarm, frighten, panic, scare, shock, stun, surprise

Really stink: disgust, offend the nose, pong, reek, repulse

Really suit: agree with, become, flatter, look good on, match

Really support: back, bankroll, encourage, endorse, promote

Really surprise: astonish, flabbergast, dumbfound, shock, stun

Really take it easy: chill, chillax, doze, idle, laze, loaf, lounge, relax

144

Really take it slow: beware, exercise caution, proceed with care

Really talk: chatter, blather, drone on, gibber, jabber, prattle, ramble

Really teach: demonstrate, explain, expound, indoctrinate, show

Really think: assume, meditate, mull over, reckon, ruminate, weigh

Really throw: catapult, fling, heave, hurl, hurtle, launch, propel

Really touch: affect, impact, influence, inspire, motivate, move, sway

Really travel: arrow, dash, fly, pelt, shoot, speed, zip, zoom

Really trust: assume, believe, count on, depend on, expect, rely on

Really try: attempt, endeavor, seek, strive, struggle, venture

Really tuck into: demolish, devour, gobble, gorge, scoff, wolf down

Really understand: comprehend, grasp, fathom, realize, twig

Really use: abuse, exploit, prey on, take advantage of, victimize

Really want: covet, crave, hanker, hunger for, lust after, yearn for

Really watch: babysit, monitor, pursue, supervise, surveil, track

Really work (1): drudge, grind, knuckle down, labor, slog, toil

Really work (2): function, hit the target, serve, succeed, triumph

Really worry: agonize, brood, dwell on, wrestle, torment oneself

Ready to tackle a ~~really significant~~ an important exercise?

Exercise

Tracy Turkey really wanted to get beyond the fence. Farmer Dave, you see, really liked turkey for Sunday dinner, and Tracy really knew her time was up.

The previous week, Wilhelmina had disappeared, and Tracy figured she was next.

She _really_ tried hard to dig under the fence with her big turkey claws, but the dirt was too hard. She _really_ chewed hard on the fence. Drats! It wouldn't give way.

Saturday night arrived. Tracy _really_ shivered in fear when she realized that Farmer Dave would take her away soon.

But guess what, children? Farmer Dave didn't _really_ want turkey that Sunday—at least not as the main course.

<u>Suggested solution</u>

Tracy Turkey needed to get beyond the fence. Now. Farmer Dave, you see, loved turkey for Sunday dinner, and Tracy realized her time was up.

The previous week, Wilhelmina had disappeared. Tracy figured she was next.

With her big turkey claws, she struggled to dig under the fence, but the dirt was too hard. She gnawed on the wire. Drats! It wouldn't give way.

Saturday night arrived. Tracy quaked in fear when she realized that Farmer Dave would take her away soon.

But guess what, children? Farmer Dave didn't hanker for turkey that Sunday—at least not as the main course.

Notes:

~~really wanted~~ = _needed_

~~really liked~~ = _loved_

~~really knew~~ = _realized_

~~really tried~~ = _struggled_

~~really chewed~~ = _gnawed_

~~really shivered~~ = _quaked_

~~really want~~ = _hanker for_

Because this is fiction for children, many writers will insist that repetition of words such as _really_ is not only permissible, but desirable.

An opposing camp argues that adults shouldn't talk down to children. These authors insist that well-written literature should be the core of each child's learning process.

You decide.

But consider this: Repetition of words such as *really* may make your work seem childish. If that's your aim, bravo. If not, perhaps it's time to reevaluate your writing.

Sad

Emotion in writing captivates readers.

But not so much if Mary Sue is *sad* on every page.

So how can a writer maintain mood without losing readers?

By *showing* emotion or replacing *sad* with other adjectives. This chapter provides the tools.

Beware the redundancy trap.

What a ~~sad~~ and tragic life Mary Sue led.

Most thesauruses list *sad* as a synonym for *tragic*. Why burden readers with two words that mean the same thing?

What a tragic life Mary Sue led.

Sad should also be removed from the following phrases and others like them—except in dialogue, which should seem natural:

Hard ~~and sad~~ times

~~Sad and~~ disappointed

~~Sad and~~ grave

~~Sad and~~ lonely

~~Sad and~~ sorry

~~Sad and~~ upset

~~Sad and~~ troubled

~~Sad~~ demise

~~Sad~~ disappointment

~~Sad~~ disaster

~~Sad~~ funeral

~~Sad~~ obituary

~~Sad,~~ gloomy countenance

Did you notice that many of the previous phrases include *and?* Keep that in mind as you edit your work.

Show your characters' sadness.

They might exhibit various behaviors, including:

Lack of energy

Empty stare

Quiet actions

Biting the lip

Clouded thoughts

Hanging the head

Downcast gaze

Monotone voice

Voice that breaks

Slouched posture

Trembling chin

Hunched shoulders

Furrowed forehead

Plodding movements

Tears or open weeping

Covering face with hands

Sitting with head in hands

Damp, red, or swollen eyes

Clenched jaw and/or stomach

Shuffling gait, with hands in pockets

Let's review a few examples.

Example 1

Dad had a long, fulfilling life, and he wouldn't want us to be _sad_ for him now that he's gone.

There's nothing wrong with this sentence, especially if it's dialogue, but we could eliminate *sad:*

Dad had a long, fulfilling life, and he wouldn't want us to mourn for him now that he's gone.

Whenever an adjective appears with *to be* (*am, are, is, was, were, will be,* etc.), the narrative suffers. In this case, I swapped *to be sad* with the more active *to mourn.*

Example 2

Justine shut the front door. Her parents knew from her _sad_ look that she had lost the election.

Knew filters the action through the senses of Justine's parents. Let's try a different approach:

Justine clicked the front door shut and murmured in monotone to her parents, "I lost the election."

Note the indications of sadness. Justine clicks the front door shut—a quiet action. Her monotone voice adds to the scene, as does her dialogue.

Example 3

With a _sad_ expression, Jordan picked up the smashed cell phone.

Nothing in the preceding sentence *shows* the degree of Jordan's emotion.

A smashed cell phone might evoke a mild response if it has been backed up recently or doesn't contain any important data. However, let's assume the phone holds irreplaceable photos of a loved one who has passed away; that would cause a strong reaction:

Chin trembling, Jordan picked up the smashed cell phone. He wept.

Is there any doubt now about the depth of Jordan's sadness?

Example 4

Maria's sad eyes made Charlie feel compassionate.

Feel is a filter word. We can edit this sentence to create a short but effective alternative:

Maria's anguished eyes filled Charlie with compassion.

Same number of words, stronger adjective, more active sentence.

Example 5

Amy was sad, so Mommy dried her tears.

Why is Amy sad? If we *show* the situation that caused the tears, we don't need *sad:*

The space under the Christmas tree was empty. Santa's milk and cookies still lay on the mantel, uneaten. Amy cried, and Mommy dried her tears.

A few extra words convey pathos that could be the basis for several paragraphs or an entire chapter.

Example 6

Roger was sad because the bank wouldn't lend him any money.

This sentence is pure *tell.*

Roger hung up the phone and slouched into his chair. "What should I do now? The bank won't approve my loan."

In the edited version, the power of dialogue combined with Roger's slouch *show* his sadness.

Replace hackneyed phrases.

Here are a few:

Sad as it might be: tragically

Sad fate: tragic demise

Sad sack: failure, dud

Sad state of affairs: upsetting situation

Sad to say: regrettably, unfortunately

If you're stuck, investigate these instant *sad* alternatives.

Some are colloquial—appropriate for dialogue or conversational narrative. Heed subtleties of meaning.

A
Agonized, anguished

B
Bereft, beside oneself with grief, bitter, bleak, blue, broken, brokenhearted, brooding, bummed out

C
Cast down, cheerless, close to tears, crestfallen, crying one's eyes out, crushed

D
Defeated, deflated, dejected, demoralized, depressed, desolate, despairing, despondent, devastated, disappointed, disconsolate, discouraged, disenchanted, disheartened, disillusioned, dismal, dismayed, dispirited, distraught, distressed, doleful, dolorous, down, down in the dumps, down in the mouth, downcast, downhearted

F
Feeling blue, forlorn, fretful, full of sorrow, funereal

G
Gloomy, glum, gone to pieces, grave, grief-stricken, grieved, gutted

H
Heartbroken, heartsick, heavyhearted, hurting

Have
Have a lump in the throat, have a bleeding heart, have a sinking heart, have an aching heart, have the blahs, have the blues

I
In a funk, in doldrums, in grief, in low spirits, in pain, in the dumps, in the pits, in the toilet, inconsolable

K
Kicking oneself

L
Let down, losing heart, losing hope, low, low-spirited, lugubrious

M
Melancholy, miserable, mopey, morbid, morose, mournful

O
On a downer, overcome with sorrow

P
Pensive

R
Reduced to tears

S
Sepulchral, sick at heart, singing the blues, somber, sorrowful, spiritless, subdued

T
Taken down, tearful, tormented, torn-up, tortured, troubled

U
Unglued, unhappy, unsettled, upset

W
Wistful, withdrawn, wretched, woebegone, woeful, worried, wretched

Ready to flex your writing muscles?

Remove all instances of *sad* from the following.

<u>Exercise 1</u>

Jessie's heart thumped like a drum in her chest. She felt <u>sad</u>, devastated. Three years. Three years she had devoted to Steve. And for what? How could he have done this to her?

<u>Suggested solution</u>

Jessie's chin trembled. Three years. Thirty-six months. One hundred fifty-six weeks. She had laughed at Steve's inane jokes, picked up his stinky socks, and listened to him snore all night. And for what? How could he have left her for another woman?

Notes: Rather than *tell* how Jessie feels, we *show* her trembling chin, and we provide a specific reason for her emotion. We also *show* some of her three-year devotion. Breaking the years into months and then into weeks emphasizes the passage of time.

<u>Exercise 2</u>

Travis was <u>sad</u>. Cardboard boxes full of memories lay on the bedroom carpet. Family photos. Benny's christening gown. Benny's baseball mitt. Travis's <u>sad</u> eyes rested on the <u>saddest</u> memory of all: Benny's baby book. *Benny. Gone forever.*

<u>Suggested solution</u>

Travis slouched into the bedroom. Cardboard boxes brimming with memories blanketed the carpet: family photos, Benny's christening gown, Benny's baseball mitt. He rubbed his swollen eyes and stared, heartsick, at his son's baby book. He sobbed. *Benny. Gone forever.*

Notes: Travis's slouching *shows* his sadness. *Brimming* is a more appropriate choice than *full of*. Slight punctuation changes strengthen readability. Travis's sad eyes are *shown* by their swollen condition, and his sob reinforces his sadness.

Exercise 3

George could tell that Janet was <u>sad</u>, but he didn't know how to comfort her. Women scared him, especially independent women who refused to let him buy them dinner. <u>Sadness</u> engulfed him. How could he ever let her know his true feelings?

Suggested solution

George squirmed in his seat. Janet's damp eyes filled him with unease. Women scared him, especially independent women who refused to let him pay for their dinner. "Is ev-everything o-okay?" He bit his lip. *Can't even talk straight. How can I ever let her know my true feelings?*

Notes: George's squirming emphasizes his unease, and his internal monologue *shows* the sadness that engulfs him. Janet's damp eyes *show* her emotion.

Exercise 4

It was <u>sad</u> when the old lady coughed. I think her name was Margaret. Or maybe Minnie? Minnie. Yeah. Every time I heard her hork her lungs out, I felt <u>sad</u>. She worked hard—harder than any of the guys—in this dungeon of a Thipakrisian mine. I often wondered as I tossed and turned in my bed at night if we'd ever get back to Earth. The <u>sad</u> fact is that if we didn't, I'd end up just like her in a few years. That <u>saddened</u> me most of all.

Suggested solution

Whenever the old lady coughed, my gut clenched. I think her name was Margaret. Or maybe Minnie? Minnie. Yeah. Every time she horked her lungs out, I wanted to cry. She worked hard—harder than any of the guys—in this dungeon of a Thipakrisian mine. I often wondered as I lay awake at night, staring at nothing, if we'd ever get back to Earth. Then, the scratching in my throat would remind me that if we didn't escape, I'd end up just like her in a few years. Frandelstax!

Notes: The narrator's clenched gut *shows* his sadness. Ditto for his desire to cry, emphasized further by his lying awake at night, staring at nothing. *Frandelstax*—nothing like an invented sci-fi expletive to augment the ambience.

Sexy

Before we mull over ways to replace *sexy*, we need to know what it means.

If you discuss this with others, you'll find varying opinions. That's part of what makes *sexy* a weak adjective. However, you have alternatives.

Writers can *show* a character's sex appeal.

Consider a few details that might make a character appear sexy to readers.

Independence: Women are less likely to date a mama's boy than an independent man who makes his own decisions; and many men are drawn to powerful women with their own careers.

Intelligence: In the early 21st century, English added a word for someone who is turned on by intelligence: *sapiosexualist*. Even so-called normal people regard intelligence as a desirable trait. Have you ever tried to converse with someone who didn't know the difference between *Botox* and *boutique*? Did you enjoy the experience?

Sense of humor: Many women are excited by brooding bad boys, but they still appreciate a sense of humor. Who wants to be serious all the time?

Joie de vivre: Those who manifest an exuberant enjoyment of life transmit an enthusiasm that infects everyone around them. Their smiles brighten a room.

Positive outlook: Wouldn't you rather share a meal with a positive person than with a pessimist? Most people would, and your characters should reflect that—unless your story features a dysfunctional person who pursues atypical relationships.

Confidence: Self-assurance outshines good looks. Some of the world's most attractive people are insecure, and love based on appearance often morphs into a dysfunctional relationship. Imbue your sexy characters with confidence.

Rolled-up sleeves on men: While a shirtless man might be overt in his sexiness, partially bared arms illustrate the allure of the classic *you shouldn't show too much skin* advice.

High heels for women, uniforms for men: These represent sexiness for most people. But maybe your protagonist was attacked by a woman in high heels or a man in uniform. Take the normal and twist it into a story.

Clothing that hides more than it reveals: What's sexier: seeing the naked body—or imagining it? Imagination is a powerful tool. Exploit it. Modesty is hot.

Good conversational skills: Someone who can maintain engaging dialogue is more appealing to both sexes than the mindless sycophant who laughs at everything the other person says.

Good personal hygiene: Most people are repelled by stinky bodies, wax-filled ears, and clothes that look like they've been slept in for weeks. Poor hygiene might be appropriate for a thug, but not for a sexy protagonist.

Dimples: Babies have dimples, and almost everyone loves babies. Dimples make a person look happy; happy implies a good sense of humor; happy people with a good sense of humor attract others.

Well-groomed hair: Hair that looks and smells clean says "I take care of myself. I'm a confident person." It doesn't have to be an elaborate hairstyle—just something that broadcasts a feeling of self-worth.

Facial symmetry: Many scientists theorize that our affinity for symmetrical faces in both men and women evolved from a desire to find a healthy mate. Although the theory is debated, facial symmetry does rate high on the scale of sexual attractiveness.

Excellent health: This attribute stems from the biological urge to find a mate who can engender healthy offspring. Even though characters may opt not to be parents, the urge will drive many of their decisions.

Sturdy physique: A sturdy physique implies excellent health and confidence.

Clear skin: Another indicator of healthiness.

Pleasant voice: Both sexes shun high, tinny voices. Try *smoky, raspy, husky, gravelly, silky, smooth, silvery, deep, velvety*, et al.

Courage: Those with courage defend their friends, lovers, and causes. What's sexier than having someone stand between you and the world when you're experiencing a bad day?

Individuality: Most people don't want a significant other who looks and acts like everyone else. Replace the cookie-cutter characters with real personalities who possess unique qualities and quirks.

Knowledge that another person is attracted to you: The heart beats faster when someone reciprocates love. Affirmation is often revealed via subtle clues like secretive glances, "accidental" touches of the hand, or blushing.

Openness and willingness to share secrets: Baring one's soul to another demonstrates trust and vulnerability. That kindles the protective instinct.

Honesty: This is closely related to the previous point. Honesty endears us to others. An unknown author once said that "the vulnerability honesty requires isn't something everybody can handle. Lying allows people to be comfortable."

Maintaining eye contact: Those who maintain eye contact with others are usually honest individuals who can be trusted. An exception: sociopaths. Story idea?

Eyes that "see into a person's soul": Your characters' eyes should be more than winking orbs with fluttering lashes.

Compassionate personality: Those who demonstrate compassion for people, animals, and the environment will do the same for their love interests.

Good listening skills: While confidence is attractive, chatter without giving anyone else a chance to talk is not—especially when the chatter is narcissistic.

Attentiveness: Does your character notice when a date's coffee needs refilling, or recognize the signs of unhappiness after a bad day at work? Sexy.

Courtesy and respect for others: Those who exhibit courtesy and respect for others will do the same for lovers.

Ethics: People with good ethics treat their sweethearts with respect, and they are less likely to cheat.

Loyalty: Someone who sticks by you no matter the circumstances is more appealing than an attractive cheater.

Politeness: Politeness means remembering a date's name, speaking in turn, and not talking with a mouth full of food. Flirting with someone else? Verboten.

Non-smoker: Sorry, smokers. Unless you hook up with another smoker, you're unlikely to make points with your addiction. The percentage of people in North America who smoke is about 15%. A smoker's dating options become smaller every year.

Someone who appreciates you at all times: "That's all right, honey. I don't mind burnt toast." "I love you, even though you stink like a barnyard right now." "Another speeding ticket? Aw, you look cute when you're embarrassed."

Humongous bank account: According to Maslow, physiological and safety needs are the two strongest motivators for all humans. A logical byproduct is a desire to pair with people who possess the financial resources to satisfy those needs.

Do you learn best by example?

Let's analyze a few snippets.

Example 1

Helene put on sexy lingerie. Burt gulped.

What makes the lingerie sexy? Whose point of view is represented? Let's make it Helene's:

Helene slipped into a sheer negligee. She smoothed her fingers over the silk, and smiled when Burt gasped.

The second paragraph *shows* interaction between the two characters, and Burt's gasp is more forceful than a gulp. In this context, *slipped into* describes Helene's donning of her negligee better than *put on*.

A few changes can communicate this from Burt's point of view:

Heat flashed into every one of Burt's extremities as Helene slipped into a sheer negligee. She smoothed her fingers over the silk, and smiled when he gasped.

Burt's reaction *shows* readers that this paragraph is from his point of view.

<u>Example 2</u>

A <u>sexy</u> man nursing a drink sat in a dark corner of the bar. Carmen walked toward him.

What makes the man sexy? Do you feel any heat or anticipation? I don't.

A man with a confident smile sat in a dark corner of the bar. His rolled-up sleeves revealed muscular arms that ended in masculine hands wrapped around a half-finished drink. Carmen's heart beat a little faster as she sidled up to him.

A brief description *shows* what Carmen considers sexy in the man. Her reaction reinforces her opinion, and *sidled up to* produces a stronger image than *walked toward*.

Let's try another version:

A brooding Marine with a neatly trimmed mustache sat erect in a dark corner of the bar, his half-finished drink clutched in a white-knuckled grip. Carmen held her breath. This was the man she dreamed about every night.

Brooding, uniform, good grooming—all *sexy* indicators for many women. Added to the mix is a bit of intrigue. Why is the Marine familiar to Carmen, and why is he clutching his drink so tightly?

<u>Example 3</u>

Every male in the room watched Miranda when she came through the door. She is so <u>sexy</u>, Marianne thought, desperate for attention.

This example provides some *show* in the first sentence, but the second is pure *tell*; and readers will be confused when they encounter characters with similar names. Time for a rewrite:

Every male in the room gawked like a lovesick schoolboy at Miranda when she sashayed through the door. Curves, flawless skin, confident smile— Venus de Milo in the flesh. Lois bit her bottom lip.

Do I need to point out the words that *show* Miranda's sexiness? Note the strong verbs *gawked* and *sashayed*. Lois's lip-biting *shows* her desperation.

Another version might amplify the tension by revealing Lois's thoughts:

Every male in the room ogled Miranda when she flounced through the door. Lois was sure the temperature jumped at least five degrees when they all rushed to join her. Blast it, she thought, why did I even bother to put on makeup? Miranda always hogs the limelight.

More strong verbs with *ogled* and *flounced*. Not a single occurrence of *sexy*, but readers will see Miranda's sexiness.

A list of adjectives to replace *sexy:*

Margaret Wolfe Hungerford said "Beauty is in the eye of the beholder." If you've exhausted all avenues to *show* sexiness, check these alternatives.

<u>A</u>
Alluring, ambrosial, arousing

<u>B</u>
Beguiling, bewitching, bodacious, bootylicious, built, busty, buxom

<u>C</u>
Captivating, chic, come-hither, coquettish, coy, curvaceous, curvy

<u>D</u>
Delectable, delicious, desirable

<u>E</u>
Enchanting, enrapturing, enthralling, enticing, entrancing, exciting, exquisite, eyesome

<u>F</u>
Feminine, fiery, flirtatious, foxy

<u>H</u>
Hot, hot-blooded, hunky

<u>I</u>
Inveigling, inviting, irresistible

J
Juicy

K
Kittenish

L
Lip-smacking, luscious, lush

M
Magnetic, masculine, mesmerizing, mouthwatering

N
Nubile

O
Oogley

P
Passionate, provocative

R
Ravishing, red-hot, riveting

S
Saucy, scrumptious, seductive, sensual, sizzling, smoking, smoky, snappy, snazzy, sniptious, spicy, stacked, steamy, stunning, suave, succulent, sultry

T
Tantalizing, tasty, tempting, titillating, torrid

V
Vampish, voluptuous

W
Well-built

Y
Yummy

Sigh of Relief

Do your protagonists sigh in relief or breathe sighs of relief on every second page? Maybe it's time for a rewrite.

Study the following example:

Ted *breathed a sigh of relief.*

A writer might make the following changes:

Ted *was relieved.*

Ted *stopped worrying.*

Ted *calmed down.*

Ted *regained his composure.*

The edited examples represent subtle differences in meaning, and they're pure *tell*. We could do better.

Investigate alternative body language.

We already know that Ted is relieved. We could *show* with body language such as:

A tentative smile

Fist-pumping

A huge exhalation of pent-up breath

Thin laughter

Holding a hand over the chest

Thanking God

Making the Sign of the Cross

Collapsing into a chair or onto a sofa

Staggering back a step to lean on something

Looking up in silent prayer

Eyes brightening and/or widening

Mopping away perspiration

Dropping to knees and clasping hands together

Raising chin and cupping back of head in hands

Making a face-palm

Closing the eyes and tilting the head back

Squaring shoulders and making a positive remark

Widening the eyes and leaning forward

Reaching for/running toward a missing person/pet

Leaning forward to hold head in hands

Raising palms toward sky or ceiling

Shedding joyful tears

Making a thumbs-up gesture

Offering a hand for a high-five

Clapping

Raising one hand in a V-for-Victory sign

Hugging anyone within reach

Dialogue to the rescue:

Sometimes a single word will *show* relief. An exclamation point can reinforce it.

"Finally!"

"Hooray!"

"Phew!"

"Whew!"

"Whoopee!"

"Woohoo!"

"Yes!"

Ration the exclamation points, though. They lose their effectiveness if they appear too frequently.

Remember that *showing* instead of *telling* usually increases word count.

In the midst of an action scene, sentences should be short and concise. *Showing* might not be the best option. However, well-chosen phrases elsewhere can energize writing.

Ready for a few examples?

Example 1

Ted <u>breathed a sigh of relief</u>. Susan blushed with embarrassment when she noticed his concern.

In addition to including a sigh of relief, the above paragraph illustrates a classic example of head-hopping. Ted can't know that Susan is embarrassed, and Susan can't know that Ted is relieved. A better approach is to pick a point-of-view character and relate events via that person's perspective.

Let's pick Ted, since he's the one who breathed the sigh of relief:

Ted grabbed Susan and pulled her in for a crushing embrace. "Where were you? I was worried."

She blushed. "I'm sorry. I didn't realize how late it was."

Zero head-hopping.

However, POV still isn't clear. Let's edit to clarify:

Ted grabbed Susan and pulled her in for a hug, but the stench of cigarette smoke made him sneeze. "Where were you? I was worried."

She blushed. "I'm sorry. I didn't realize how late it was."

Now we know that Ted is the POV character, because we experience what he smells; and with a few extra words, we've added tension. Has Susan been sneaking cigarettes behind his back?

<u>Example 2</u>

The entire USA <u>breathed a sigh of relief</u> when everyone realized that President Reagan had survived the assassination attempt.

Exaggeration has its place in fiction, but not in accounts of factual events. A better approach would be to set up a scene in a public place and *show* the reactions of a few people:

Everyone in the bar stared at the TV next to the jukebox as Frank Reynolds of ABC News announced that President Reagan had survived the assassination attempt.

Thin laughter sounded from one patron. Another made the Sign of the Cross. A third slammed his fist onto the table and mumbled, "Great, another three years with a stupid actor in charge of the country."

This is a more realistic scenario. Two people *show* relief, but one demonstrates dissatisfaction with the outcome.

<u>Example 3</u>

Ray <u>breathed a sigh of relief</u>. "So, doctor, you're telling me all the cancer is gone? I'm gonna live?"

A sigh of relief could be an understatement here. Ray might even be incapable of speech for a moment, because his death sentence has been revoked:

Ray's eyes filled with tears, and he collapsed onto the floor of the doctor's office. All the cancer was gone. He was going to live!

The second example *shows* a stronger reaction—appropriate for the situation.

Ray staggered back a step. Two. He held a hand over his chest. All the cancer was gone. He had his life back!

Although too much body language can dilute rather than amplify, an occasion like this might warrant it.

Example 4

Evan stepped onto the scale. He <u>breathed a sigh of relief</u>. Two pounds to go, ten days left. He could do this.

A smile might work here, but let's create a more dramatic scenario:

Evan stepped onto the scale and exhaled a huge pent-up breath. Two pounds to go, ten days left. He could do this.

If those two pounds represent Evan's goal to fit into a suit for his wedding, he might exhibit even stronger body language:

Even stepped onto the scale. Two pounds to go, ten days left. He pumped his fist. Yes! He could do this.

Isn't the fist pump more effective than a sigh of relief?

Short alternatives for *breathe a sigh of relief*:

Beware.

Most of these are *tells,* and some are cliché. Others incorporate filter words that distance readers from narrative.

<u>B</u>
Become encouraged, breathe easy/easily, buck up

<u>C</u>
Calm down, cheer up, chillax, collect oneself, compose oneself, cool down

<u>F</u>
Feel happy, feel optimistic, feel relieved, feel secure, find the answer, find the key, find the solution, forget one's anxiety

<u>G</u>
Gather the wits, get a grip on oneself, get control of one's anxiety, get hold of oneself, get one's act together

<u>L</u>
Loosen up

<u>M</u>
Mellow out

P
Perk up, pull oneself together

Q
Quieten

R
Rally, regain composure, regain self-control, regroup, relax, rest easier

S
See the light at the end of the tunnel, settle down, simmer down, snap out of it, steady oneself, stop being frightened, stop worrying

U
Unwind

W
Wind down

Exercises and story prompts:

Eliminate sighs of relief in the following.

Exercise 1

Republicans breathed a collective <u>sigh of relief</u> when Trump said he'd stop tweeting. Their relief turned into anxiety at 3 a.m. the next morning.

Exercise 2

A gas station—finally. Scott exhaled a <u>sigh of relief</u>. *Phew! I'm running on fumes.* His car lurched to within a few yards of the pumps, and then coughed to a stop. Attempts to restart the engine failed.

He beat one fist against the steering wheel before climbing out.

A tumbleweed drifted between the station and the pumps. A sun-faded sign in the side window advertised BYE ONE CHOCKLATE BAR GET 1 FREE. Tall grass swayed in the cracks of the cement. *Must have been years since this dump was painted.* "Hello? Is anyone here? Hello?"

A petite blonde stepped into view. Scott heaved a <u>sigh of relief</u>. *Curves in all the right places. But those eyes ...* Opaque blue orbs stared through him as though he didn't exist. The woman shuffled toward him, silent except for the scrape of her feet over the cement.

Scott turned and ran.

Exercise 3

Fritz exhaled a <u>sigh of relief</u>. Fourteen days lost in the forest. Now, he faced a lavish meal that his loving wife had prepared. Would he be able to digest it?

He bowed his head in silent prayer, thanking God for the food and showing him the way home to Edwina.

He took a tentative bite and chewed slowly. *Mmm. Ambrosia.* Another <u>sigh of relief</u> ascended to Heaven. The next mouthful vanished with nary a chew. Before long, the remainder of the food disappeared, as Fritz gnawed and growled like a caged bear.

All too soon his plate was bare. He belched. A good belch. A belch tinged with the taste and scent of ... *No!*

Exercise 4

Numbers scrolled across the display at the front of the class, cuing a <u>sigh of relief</u> from Acker Space Academy students. Nobody had failed. In fact, they had all graduated with perfect scores.

A buzz of excitement spread through the room.

"All of us? Impossible."

"How could it be?"

"Is this a joke?"

A grim-faced proctor stomped into view. "Willis, Mellinger, and Einstein, report to Admiral Arquette. Immediately."

Use

How often do you use the verb *use*?

Use, make *use* of, put to *use*.

Use a key, *use* a credit card, *use* a language.

This three-letter word haunts public signs.

It hangs out in instruction manuals, and we *use* our outside voices to curse the idiocy of the people who wrote the manuals.

Worst of all, *use* appears so often in some books that we want to *use* a match to incinerate them.

This chapter presents dozens of ways to mitigate *use* abuse.

Straightforward replacements often solve the problem.

Review the following sentences. Is *use* the best choice for each situation? Other words deliver connotations that might prove better:

Accept
~~Use~~ Accept someone's help.

Apply
~~Use~~ Apply makeup.

Benefit from
~~Use~~ Benefit from the library.

Demonstrate
~~Use~~ Demonstrate good manners.

Employ
~~Use~~ Employ techniques.

Exercise
~~Use~~ Exercise good judgment.

Follow
~~Use~~ Follow a recipe.

Hire
~~Use~~ Hire a personal trainer.

Initiate
~~Use~~ Initiate a procedure.

Offer
~~Use~~ Offer as collateral.

Operate
~~Use~~ Operate tools.

Rely on
~~Use~~ Rely on a computer.

Wield
~~Use~~ Wield a gun.

Rather than replace *use,* **consider alternative wording, including clichés if appropriate:**

Use a credit card
Buy on credit, swipe the stripe, make MasterCard moan

Use a key
Access, gain entry, open, unlock

Use a language
Speak in/write in/communicate in _____ [name of language]

Use a microphone
Amplify the voice, speak into a microphone, blast the audience's ears

Use a paintbrush
Coat, dab, daub, decorate, paint, smear, splatter, whitewash

Use a pen
Draw, endorse, jot down, note, pen, print, scribble, sign, write

Use a phone
Buzz, call, dial, get on the blower, phone, ring, telephone

Use a trash bag
Bundle/throw into a trash bag, discard, garbage, throw away, trash

Use as a weapon
Convert into a weapon, threaten with, weaponize

Use as an excuse
Blame something, make excuses, pin on, point the finger at

Use common sense
Consider before acting, exercise prudence, practice caution

Use drugs
Dope, drop, drug, get high, inject, mainline, shoot up, snort

Use elbow grease
Apply oneself, exert oneself, knuckle down, persevere, work hard

Use every trick in the book
Boil the ocean, do anything to succeed, go all-out, strive, try hard

Use fertilizer
Compost, dress, enrich the soil, feed, fertilize, mulch, top-dress

Use foul language
Blaspheme, curse, cuss, swear, utter profanities, turn the air blue

Use good judgment
Choose wisely, exercise caution, harness one's horse sense, succeed

Use magic
Bewitch, cast a spell, curse, enchant, hex, possess

Use one's fist
Batter, clout, cold-cock, fist, pound, pummel, punch, strike, wallop

Use one's hands.
Operate by hand, perform manually; act out, gesture, pantomime, sign, signal

Use one's head
Contemplate, deliberate, meditate, mull over, reason, think, weigh

Use one's loaf
Figure out by oneself, think smart, work smarter not harder

Use one's teeth
Bite, champ, chew, chomp, gnaw, masticate, munch, nibble

Use over
Recondition, recycle, reprocess, reuse, reutilize, salvage

Use poor judgment
Botch, err, fail, flop, flub, foul up, make a mess, mess up, spoil

Use soap
Bathe, clean, cleanse, lather, launder, scrub, shower, soap, wash

Use (somebody or something)
Abuse, exploit, manipulate, stage-manage, take advantage of

Use subterfuge
Con, deceive, dupe, evade, fake, hoodwink, lie, mislead, swindle, trick

Use sugar
Add sugar, candify, candy, mull, sugar, sweeten

Use the best china
Brag, hide the dirty laundry, make a good impression, posture, show off

Use the car
Chauffeur, drive, motor, putt-putt, tailgate, weave through traffic

Use torture
Assault, beat, brutalize, lay into, punish, torment, torture

Use up
Consume, deplete, drain, eat up, empty, exhaust, expend, finish

Replace the modal verb-phrase *used to*.

Used to typically precedes an infinitive:

Used to swim

Used to walk

Used to read

Try swapping the modal with words and phrases such as:

Always

Formerly

In the old days

In the past

Once

Once upon a time

Previously

When dinosaurs roamed the Earth

When he was a kid

When she was younger

Whenever I _____

Would

Run careful search-and-replace operations.

Determine intended meaning before choosing any of the following alternatives. Many will steer creativity in new directions. Embrace them as opportunities to add subplots or to augment details of narrative.

A
Accept, activate, actuate, administer, apply, arrange, avail oneself of

B
Begin, benefit from, brandish, bring about, bring into play, bring on, bring to bear, burn through

C
Capitalize on, carry out, carry through, cash in on, cause, channel, commence, conduct, consume, control, coordinate

D
Demonstrate, depend on, deplete, deploy, develop, devour, disburse, draw on, drive

E
Eat up, effectuate, employ, empty, energize, engage, engender, establish, execute, exercise, exert, exhaust, expend, exploit

F
Finish, flaunt, flourish, follow, fulfill

H
Handle, harness, have recourse to, hire

I
Ignite, implement, initiate, instigate

L
Leverage

M
Manage, maneuver, manipulate, mobilize

N
Negotiate

O
Offer, operate, orchestrate, organize, originate

P
Perform, pioneer, ply, practice, prepare, put forth, put into action, put into effect, put into operation, put into service

R
Rely on, resort to, run

S
Spark, spearhead, spend, start, steer

T
Take on, trigger

U
Utilize

W
Wield, work, work with

Time to ~~use~~ wield your red pencil:

Reduce or eliminate *use, used,* and *used to.*

<u>Exercise</u>

"<u>Use</u> your imagination," said Mrs. Peters as she held a beaker against the classroom window. Sunlight filtered through murky liquid and illuminated tiny moving objects. "What could they be?"

A boy near the door <u>used</u> a finger to tap ~~away~~ for a few seconds on his cell phone. "Baby shrimp?"

"No."

A girl in the back row piped up, "I <u>used to</u> get tadpoles from the pond near our house every spring. They kinda look like that."

"No, they're not tadpoles. <u>Use</u> your heads. What have we been discussing in class for the last two days?"

Almost as one, the class chorused, "Aliens."

Mrs. Peters <u>used</u> an index finger to push her glasses onto the bridge of her nose. The sunlight filtered through her neck and jaw now, illuminating bones and muscles.

<u>Suggested solution</u>

"Look—and imagine," said Mrs. Peters as she held a beaker against the classroom window. Sunlight filtered through murky liquid and illuminated tiny moving objects. "What could they be?"

A boy near the door tapped for a few seconds on his cell phone. "Baby shrimp?"

"No."

A girl in the back row piped up, "When I was little, I got tadpoles from the pond near our house every spring. They kinda look like that."

"No, they're not tadpoles. Think. What have we been discussing in class for the last two days?"

Almost as one, the class chorused, "Aliens."

Mrs. Peters pushed her glasses onto the bridge of her nose. The sunlight filtered through her neck and jaw now, illuminating bones and muscles.

Notes:

Use your imagination becomes *Look—and imagine,* which is appropriate, since Mrs. Peters holds something up for the class to observe.

A boy near the door used a finger to tap away becomes *A boy near the door tapped.* There's no need to *show* him using a finger. Readers will envision that without the extra words.

I used to get tadpoles from the pond is reworded to *When I was little, I got tadpoles from the pond.* The edited version helps establish that the girl was probably a preschooler when she did this.

Use your heads becomes *Think.*

Mrs. Peters used an index finger to push her glasses onto the bridge of her nose becomes *Mrs. Peters pushed her glasses onto the bridge of her nose.* As with the boy on his cell phone, readers will assume she uses a finger. If she had pushed her glasses with a piece of chalk or another object that has some bearing on this scene, including it would be appropriate. Otherwise, the extra words contribute nothing.

Why has the class been discussing aliens? Maybe the students can see an alien growing inside Mrs. Peters. Does she have two tongues, perhaps?

Wink

Do your characters wink so often that their eyes resemble flashing signal lights?

Onlookers could perceive a wink in many ways. For instance, they might deem it friendly, creepy, lecherous, or sinister.

As you write and edit, ask a key question:

Why do your characters wink? Knowing the reason will help you choose alternatives.

Common causes include:

Amusement, confidence, flirtatiousness, jocularity, reassurance, secrecy or shared knowledge, sympathy

Try some of the following actions to replace winks.

Amusement
Snorting
Loud laughter
Making joking comments
Suppressing giggles

Confidence
Thumbs-up
Bright smile
Robust handshake
Meeting everyone's gaze

[Exercise caution with the thumbs-up gesture. In some African countries, Australia, the Middle East, Japan, and certain areas of Europe, people will interpret it as an insult.]

Flirtatiousness
Coy smile
Tossing the hair
Touching or stroking someone's arm
Sweeping the gaze over another person's body

Jocularity
Bright eyes
Impish grin
Jovial banter
Exuberant laughter

Reassurance
Friendly hug
Positive dialogue
Volunteering assistance
Offering coffee, tea, or alcoholic beverages

Secrecy or shared knowledge
Sending private text messages
Whispering with another character
Exchanging knowing glances with someone
Laying a *please-don't-tell* finger against the lips

Sympathy
Sad smile
Comforting dialogue
Patting someone's back or shoulder
Murmuring optimistic platitudes in a soothing tone

You'll find other actions and motivations if you search the internet for *body language wink.*

Let's roll up our virtual writing sleeves and replace a few winks.

Example 1

Jasmine grinned and <u>winked</u>.

We see no indication of Jasmine's motivation, although the grin provides direction.

Jasmine exchanged a knowing glance with Wade.

Jasmine and Wade obviously share a secret.

Jasmine tossed her hair and smiled coyly at Wade.

This time Jasmine is flirting with Wade. Although excessive use of adverbs weakens writing, occasional words such as *coyly* reduce exposition.

<u>Example 2</u>

Celeste <u>winked</u> as she turned toward the living room.

Celeste's wink is probably a response to an event that just happened—perhaps something funny?

Celeste smothered a laugh as she turned toward the living room.

This provides a distinct image we don't see in the first sentence, and it clarifies her motivation.

Celeste gave Maurice a warm hug and then turned toward the living room.

A warm hug represents the epitome of friendship. Maybe Maurice wants more?

<u>Example 2</u>

Lacey rolled her eyes and <u>winked</u> at the professor.

Rolling the eyes suggests different motivation than winking. Why confuse readers?

Lacey met, and held, the professor's gaze.

This portrays a confident Lacey who probably knows the answer to whatever question the professor just asked. The commas emphasize her self-assurance.

Lacey gave the professor a thumbs-up.

Once again we see a confident Lacey. In North America, a thumbs-up is an informal gesture. It could indicate an after-hours relationship with a mentor.

Example 4

Amy <u>winked</u>, and devoured a sixth doughnut.

Did Amy swipe the doughnut from someone?

Amy snorted, and devoured a sixth doughnut.

Same number of words, but now we see conflict that could develop into humor or an altercation with another character.

Amy suppressed a giggle, and devoured a sixth doughnut.

This example could likewise segue into humor or a confrontation.

Example 5

Stephanie <u>winked</u> at Clarence in answer.

Is Stephanie answering a question, or responding to Clarence's actions?

Stephanie answered, "Of course, I'll go. I haven't been to Disneyland in years."

No misinterpretation here. Dialogue often provides the best way to clarify motivation.

Stephanie responded to Clarence with a bright smile.

A wink might be misunderstood, but a bright smile leaves little room for doubt.

Example 6

Tears <u>winked</u> out of Betty's eyes.

This is a nonstandard use of *wink*. Since a wink is the quick closing and reopening of one eye, the sentence doesn't make sense.

Tears flooded out of Betty's eyes.

Flooded is a better verb choice. *Streamed* or *gushed* would also work.

Betty wept.

Short. To the point. A good choice when word count is limited.

Are you guilty of these *wink* no-nos?

George <u>winked</u> ~~slowly~~.

Have you ever seen anyone wink slowly? By definition, *wink* means to close and reopen an eye *quickly*.

Ethan <u>winked</u> ~~an eye~~.

What else would Ethan wink? His mouth? Remember the definition.

Ethan <u>winked</u> ~~out of one eye~~.

Given the foregoing remark, I shouldn't need to comment on this one.

Zara <u>winked</u> uncontrollably.

A wink refers to a single action of the eyelid; therefore, multiple winks would be tics or spasmodic contractions.

Andy <u>winked</u>, "Can't you tell I was joking?"

A wink creates an action beat, not a dialogue tag. You can't wink speech; therefore, the comma in the example should be replaced by a period.

Dereck <u>winked</u> at Karen in the total darkness of the cave.

Dereck knows that Karen can't see him. Why would he wink? This would be a good place to insert whispering, stumbling over unseen obstacles, or touching the other person for reassurance.

Charles gave Marshall a <u>wink</u>.

Charles gives Marshall something. Readers might expect it to be a tangible object. The sentence could be reworded as *Charles winked at Marshall*. The change produces direct action that is less likely to pull readers out of the story.

Avoid similar phrases such as *execute a wink, bestow a wink,* and *impart a wink.*

The police sergeant <u>winked</u> at the bribes taken by constables under his command.

In this context, *winked at* means *ignored*. Although the wording is correct, readers might misunderstand it. Why not choose the unambiguous verb *ignored* instead?

Kris <u>winked</u> ~~to himself privately~~.

I doubt that Kris would be able to hide a wink, so he wouldn't wink to himself. *Privately* compounds the goof.

Maria <u>winked</u> *as she stared at the gem.*

Can you wink and stare at the same time? I can't. This would be better:

Maria winked and stared at the gem.

What about a variation?

<u>Winking</u>, *Maria stared at the gem.*

No! The present participle (*ing* form) of a verb indicates concurrent action, which is impossible in this case. As in the previous example, Maria can't simultaneously wink and stare.

Basic *wink* alternatives convey multiple nuances.

Study these examples and note the subtle differences in meaning:

Libby <u>winked</u> at Harrison.

Libby <u>batted her eyelashes</u> at Harrison.

Libby <u>blinked</u> at Harrison.

Libby <u>locked eyes</u> with Harrison.

Libby <u>nudged</u> Harrison.

Libby <u>peeked</u> at Harrison.

Libby <u>squinted</u> at Harrison.

And now, the list:

These alternatives for *wink* are convenient when a writer must conserve words.

<u>B</u>
Bat the eyelashes, blink

<u>C</u>
Cast a playful eye, crinkle the eyes

<u>E</u>
Elbow, eye, eye up, eyeball

<u>F</u>
Flirt, flicker an eyelid, flutter the eyelashes

<u>G</u>
Give a seductive look [See foregoing note about Charles giving Marshall a wink.], goggle

<u>L</u>
Leer, lock eyes

<u>M</u>
Make eyes, make sheep's eyes

<u>N</u>
Nudge

<u>O</u>
Ogle

<u>P</u>
Peek

<u>R</u>
Rubberneck

<u>S</u>
Squint

Time for practice:

Can you remove *wink* and *winked* in the following exercises?

Exercise 1

Judy's eyes flooded with tears. She reached for Nathaniel.

He <u>winked</u> at her and patted her back. "Don't worry, I won't tell anyone what you did."

[This could lead to a humorous story if Judy flubbed something at work. However, if she buried a body in the backyard, you could develop this into horror. What about a combination of humor and horror?]

Exercise 2

Only ten minutes of FaceTime. Sharon <u>winked</u> as she stared at Sean.

He <u>winked</u> back. "Let's go. Ten minutes isn't long."

[What will Sharon and Sean do in the brief time allotted? You could go for the obvious, or have them plan a robbery. Maybe Sharon needs to rehearse a speech? Remember my remarks about concurrent actions. *As* indicates that Sharon winks while she is staring.]

Exercise 3

Keith <u>winked</u> and laid his hand on Jim's arm.

Jim flinched for a moment and studied the hand before returning the <u>wink</u>.

Keith glowered. "I thought we were good. You having second thoughts?"

[Second thoughts about what?]

Overused Punctuation

Are you a punctuation junkie?

The first volume of *The Writer's Lexicon* tackled overuse of *!*, ..., and —, which provide clarity when applied well but annoy readers if overexploited.

Volume II discusses the relevance of apostrophes in contractions.

Contractions

A contraction is a shortened word or phrase with one or more apostrophes that replace(s) missing letter(s).

Contractions have been part of the English language for centuries. Nowadays even in many formal documents, occasional use is permitted. Without them, text seems stilted.

We rely on contractions in speech. Transferring that custom to our writing creates realistic narrative.

Beware of contractionitis, though.

Multiple meanings often obscure a writer's intent.

Apostrophe-d can replace *had, did,* or *would.*

Apostrophe-s might replace *is, was* (incorrect, but sometimes heard in dialogue), or *has.*

Will readers understand what lurks behind the apostrophe?

Review the following guidelines. They could help prevent confusion.

Guideline 1. When *had* indicates possession, write it in full.

He'd too many apples in the basket.

The first instinct a reader has when reading *he'd* is to expect *had* or *would* in their function as an auxiliary verb.

He had too many apples in the basket.

The edited version resolves ambiguity.

Guideline 2. When *apostrophe-s* replaces an emphatic *is* or *has*, write the verb in full.

"Jillian's going."

In this example, the speaker could be reading through a list of prospective party guests and crossing off the names of those who have confirmed.

"Jillian is going."

Here we see what could be a response to another person's insistence that Jillian won't be at the party.

Guideline 3. Eliminate confusion about verb tense.

Claire's gone.

This could be either present or past tense. Removing the contraction prevents uncertainty when context is vague.

Claire is gone.

Claire has gone.

If people have to stop even for a millisecond to puzzle over words, they become distracted. Any pause disrupts the flow. Do this too often, and you lose readers.

Guideline 4. Avoid *apostrophe-s* contractions with names or capitalized nouns.

Susan's written ...

Readers might interpret *apostrophe-s* in this situation as indicating possessive case.

The phrase could start sentences like:

Susan's written work is difficult to decipher because of her messy handwriting.

Susan's written several books about protecting the environment.

The second sentence would be better if rewritten without the *apostrophe-s:*

Susan has written several books about protecting the environment.

Dialogue is always an exception. Keep it realistic—but understandable.

Guideline 5. *Apostrophe-ve* is short for *have,* not *of.*

The full form of *should've* is *should have* not *should of.* There is no such phrase as *should of.* That also applies to *could of* and *would of.*

I <u>would've</u> gone if I had known.
I <u>would have</u> gone if I had known.

You <u>should've</u> tipped the server.
You <u>should have</u> tipped the server.

You <u>could've</u> at least tried.
You <u>could have</u> at least tried.

Yet another reminder: Dialogue should sound authentic.

Guideline 6. Avoid complex, nonstandard, or unusual contractions.

Any word or phrase that slows comprehension detracts from narrative. The following contractions and their relatives create confusion. Evaluate carefully before using them.

Yes, they are real. Google them if you need proof.

<u>Amn't:</u> am not

<u>Couldn't've:</u> could not have

<u>Hadn't've:</u> had not have

<u>He'd've:</u> he would have

<u>He'dn't've:</u> he did/would not have

<u>He'sn't:</u> he is not

<u>I'd've:</u> I did/would have

<u>I'dn't:</u> I did/had/would not

<u>I'dn't've:</u> I did/would not have

<u>I'ven't:</u> I have not

<u>It'd've:</u> it did/would have

<u>It'dn't:</u> it did/had/would not

<u>It'dn't've:</u> it did/would not have

<u>Mustn't've:</u> must not have

She'd've: she did/would have

She'dn't: she did/had/would not

She'dn't've: she did/would not have

Shouldn't've: should not have

Somebody'd've: somebody did/would have

Somebody'dn't've: somebody did/would not have

Someone'd've: someone did/would have

Someone'dn't: someone did/had/would not

Something'd've: something did/would have

Something'dn't: something did/had/would not

Something'dn't've: something did/would not have

There'd've: there would have

There'dn't: there did/had/would not

There'dn't've: there would not have

They'd've: they did/would have

They'd'ven't: they would have not

They'dn't: they did/had/would not

They'dn't've: they did/would not have

We won't've: we will not have

We'd've: we did/would have

We'dn't: we did/had/would not

We'dn't've: we did/would not have

Who'd've: who would have

Won't've: will not have

Wouldn't've: would not have

You'd've: you did/would have

Guideline 7. Note the exceptions.

If you're making a direct quote, even though the quote contains incorrect punctuation or is difficult to interpret, the misused contraction(s) should stay. This includes letters and diaries penned by characters as well as other written or quoted material, whether fictional or true.

Clichés and idioms often include contractions. Treat them as direct quotes. Platitudes like the following lose their appeal if converted to complete words:

Don't give up your day job.

Don't look a gift horse in the mouth.

Don't put all your eggs in one basket.

If it's not one thing, it's another.

It's a small world.

It's anyone's call.

You can't judge a book by its cover.

Guideline 8. Contractions do not belong in legalese.

Every word in documents such as wills, mortgages, and partnership agreements must be unambiguous. A misinterpretation could cause unintended consequences.

Read your work out loud.

Listening to your words will often pinpoint areas where contractions seem natural, and others where they don't.

Exercise caution with search-and-replace.

In your zeal to reduce the number of contractions in your work, you might be tempted to run a blanket search-and-replace.

Don't.

Examine every occurrence individually, or prepare yourself for unexpected glitches.

For example, searching for instances of *n't* and replacing with *[space] not* produces the following results:

Won't becomes *Wo not.*

Can't becomes *Ca not.*

Ain't becomes *Ai not.*

Worse yet, word flow suffers:

Why didn't you say something? becomes *Why did not you say something?*

The correct wording should be *Why did you not say something?*

More examples follow. Each set begins with the original sentence, followed by the search-and-replace result, and ending with the human-corrected version:

Aren't you coming?
Are not you coming?
Are you not coming?

Don't you think?
Do not you think?
Do you not think?

Why can't he come?
Why ca not he come?
Why can he not come?

Why hadn't he told the truth?
Why had not he told the truth?
Why had he not told the truth?

Perhaps someday scientists will develop computer algorithms that can analyze a writer's style and make appropriate decisions without human intervention.

Test your knowledge.

Correct the following sentences. Because no context is provided, base your answers on the most extreme misunderstandings readers might demonstrate.

1. Last Will and Testament've John Doe.

2. William's gone to the store.

3. I'd a banana for my mid-morning snack.

4. Connie's grown daughters.

5. No matter what Shelby says, Timmy's going.

6. A leopard cannot change its spots.

7. Something'dn't add up.

8. Many writer's sell their book's on Amazon.

1. Last Will and Testament of John Doe.

[See Guidelines 5, 6, and 8.]

2. William is/has gone to the store.

[See Guidelines 3 and 4.]

3. I had a banana for my mid-morning snack.

[See Guideline 1.]

4. Connie has grown/adult daughters.

[See Guideline 4. Even after removing the contraction, *adult* is a better word choice than *grown*.]

5. No matter what Shelby says, Timmy is/*is* going.

[See Guidelines 2, 3, and 4.]

6. A leopard can't change its spots.

[See Guideline 7.]

7. Something didn't add up.

[See Guideline 6.]

8. Many writers sell their books on Amazon.

[*Writer's* and *book's* are not contractions. They are plural forms and don't require apostrophes.]

Taboos

Writing taboos are guidelines, sometimes overlooked for the sake of creativity and reader engagement.

The first volume of *The Writer's Lexicon* discussed absolute adjectives, cursing, redundancies, first-person narrative, and other topics.

Volume II continues with no-nos such as action-beat abuse, filter words, stacked modifiers, and word bloat—embracing these so-called taboos and providing strategies for ignoring them.

Action-Beat Abuse

Effective action beats enhance dialogue.

A single action can replace many words of description. We associate a scowl with displeasure, a stomping foot with anger, and tears with sadness.

But how often do your characters shake their heads, nod, or shrug while involved in conversation? Maybe they endlessly clear their throats, pout, or sigh. Action beats, like any literary device, distract readers if abused. Overreliance on them weakens writing.

Before starting, we need to know the definition of *action beat.*

An action beat is the description of an action a character makes while talking. It may replace, or appear along with, a dialogue tag.

For example:

"Go away," Ted said. [Dialogue tag]

"Go away." Ted pointed at the door. [Action beat]

Note the difference in punctuation. A comma follows *away* in the first instance, and a period follows it in the second.

Ted's action augments the dialogue and provides a meaningful visual for readers. Some writers might prefer:

"Go away," Ted said as he pointed at the door.

However, the action beat *shows* readers that Ted is talking. Why burden the writing with unnecessary words?

Let's examine an excerpt from a short story:

Brenda frowned and shook her head. "No way. You expect me to jump out of a perfectly good plane and depend on a flimsy piece of silk to keep me from splattering into the ground?"

Mike sighed. "I've done hundreds of jumps." He cleared his throat. "Besides, parachutes are usually made out of nylon nowadays."

"Yeah, nylon." She nodded ~~her head~~. "Nylon. Nylon! Have you ever seen a run in a nylon stocking?" She shrugged ~~her shoulders~~. "Find yourself another sucker." [81 words]

Note the strikethroughs. What else would Brenda nod besides her head? What else would she shrug besides her shoulders? Four superfluous words eliminated.

Although *sucker* is cliché, it makes the dialogue seem genuine. Your speakers should sound like real people.

Each paragraph includes multiple action beats, but do we require more than one? Once the speaker is known, a single well-chosen beat will *show* emotion without adding gratuitous padding.

Do we need an action beat in the third paragraph? This is an altercation that involves two characters. Readers will know who is speaking.

With the interruption of Brenda's dialogue, the writer might not notice the repetition of *nylon*, but readers will.

Time for a rewrite:

Brenda frowned. "No way. You expect me to jump out of a perfectly good plane and depend on a flimsy piece of silk to keep me from splattering into the ground?"

Mike sighed. "I've done hundreds of jumps. Besides, parachutes are usually made out of nylon nowadays."

"Yeah, nylon. Nylon! Have you ever seen a run in a nylon stocking? Find yourself another sucker." [64 words]

Better.

However, if you scrutinize the rest of the story containing these paragraphs, you might discover ad nauseam recurrences of *frowned* and *sighed*—problem words for many writers.

How do you remedy the repetition?

Consider motivation.

Why does Brenda frown? Perhaps she's agitated. A wavering voice or erratic movements would *show* that. Maybe she's defiant. She might cock her head or fix Mike with a stony stare. Embarrassment might compel her to blush or sweat.

Why does Mike sigh? Exasperation might make him clench his fists or point his finger at Brenda. Impatience could cause pinched lips, or oblige him to throw an object at the wall. Overconfidence might result in a bellowing voice or aggressive stance.

You control the narrative. If you don't know why your protagonists are frowning or sighing, how can you expect your readers to?

Try the mirror approach: Determine motivation and stand in front of a mirror while you act out the triggering emotion. Where are your hands and feet? Are your brows arched or furrowed? Is your chin thrust forward or drawn toward your chest? Has your complexion changed color?

If you're stuck for appropriate body language, search the internet for phrases such as *body language agitation* or *body language exasperation*.

Time for a second rewrite:

Brenda's face reddened. "No way. You expect me to jump out of a perfectly good plane and depend on a flimsy piece of silk to keep me from splattering into the ground?"

"I've done hundreds of jumps." Mike tossed a pen at the wall. "Besides, parachutes are usually made out of nylon nowadays."

"Yeah, nylon. Nylon! Have you ever seen a run in a nylon stocking? Find yourself another sucker." [70 words]

The third version introduces tension. Readers will envision the red face and tossed pen, intuiting the emotions that precipitated them.

Scrutinize a second excerpt.

"They won't budge on the overtime clause." Burt, the CEO's executive assistant, grimaced and scratched his chin. "And they'll strike if we don't increase their health benefits." He paced, one hand behind his back.

The CEO sighed and leaned forward in his chair. "Scum." He dragged an expensive cigar from a desk drawer and peered at his Rolex. "Their demands will cost a fortune. They'll force us into the poorhouse."

Burt strolled across the plush carpet to the mini bar and poured himself a twenty-year-old Glenfiddich scotch whiskey. "If we lay off some of the work force, we could give them what they want." He smacked his lips and gazed out the window. "And they might not be so willing to test our resolve next time the contract comes up for renewal."

The CEO inspected his manicured nails and cleared his throat. "Do it."
[144 words]

The writer wants to communicate that the company has rich executives, but they're not willing to share their good fortune with employees.

Let's rewrite. First, we'll strike out the unnecessary beats:

"They won't budge on the overtime clause." Burt, the CEO's executive assistant, ~~grimaced and scratched his chin~~. "And they'll strike if we don't increase their health benefits." He paced~~, one hand behind his back~~.

The CEO ~~sighed and leaned forward in his chair~~. "Scum." He dragged an expensive cigar from a desk drawer and peered at his Rolex. "Their demands will cost a fortune. They'll force us into the poorhouse."

Burt strolled across the plush carpet to the mini bar and poured himself a twenty-year-old Glenfiddich scotch whiskey. "If we lay off some of the work force, we could give them what they want." ~~He smacked his lips and gazed out the window.~~ "And they might not be so willing to test our resolve next time the contract comes up for renewal."

The CEO inspected his manicured nails ~~and cleared his throat~~. "Do it."

With deletion of the indicated beats and a bit of reorganization, we can streamline the narrative:

Burt, the CEO's executive assistant, paced across the plush carpet. "They won't budge on the overtime clause. And they'll strike if we don't increase their health benefits."

"Scum." The CEO dragged an expensive cigar from a desk drawer and peered at his Rolex. "Their demands will cost a fortune. They'll force us into the poorhouse."

Burt strolled to the mini bar and poured himself a twenty-year-old Glenfiddich scotch whiskey. "If we lay off some of the work force, we could give them what they want. And they might not be so willing to test our resolve next time the contract comes up for renewal."

The CEO inspected his manicured nails. "Do it." [112 words]

Every action beat now adds to the scene.

Exploit action beats, and your writing will benefit.

Try this:

1. Save your document.

2. Strike out unnecessary beats.

3. Resave the document.

4. Reword as needed.

Ready for a few exercises?

Exercise 1

Burton shook his head and sighed. "Edwina will never believe me," he said, "no matter how much I deny it." He slumped in his chair.

Roland smiled, and his eyes twinkled. "But I have video evidence. Look here," he answered as he pointed at the screen on his phone.

"Really?" Burton asked, peering over Roland's shoulder.

"Yes." Roland brought up a video of the cat eating Edwina's prize carrot cake. "See? You're in the clear, bud."

Suggested solution

Burton slumped in his chair. "Edwina will never believe me, no matter how much I deny it."

Roland's eyes twinkled. "But I have video evidence. Look here." He pointed at the screen on his phone.

"Really?"

"Yes." Roland brought up a video of the cat eating Edwina's prize carrot cake. "See? You're in the clear, bud."

Notes: *Notes:* All dialogue tags and extraneous action beats were removed. "Really?" was left without speaker identification, because it's clear that Burton is talking.

Exercise 2

Reverend Phelps looked at the congregation as he adjusted his tie. "Good morning," he said. "I'm glad to see so many bright faces." ₀He paused.

An elderly lady in the front row raised both hands in the air and said, "Amen."

He shuffled his notes and cleared his throat. "Today I'd like to talk about the need to respect our bodies—the temples we have been granted during our short sojourn on Earth." He pushed his glasses high onto the bridge of his nose.

A collective groan went through the crowd. Every sermon for three weeks had been about the perils of drugs and strong drink. Somewhere near the back of the church, a snore sounded.

The Reverend hit his fist on the pulpit and shouted, "Today's sermon will be about the necessity of sufficient sleep every night." He pursed his lips. "I must say I am disappointed at the number of my parishioners who snooze every Sunday during church."

Suggested solution

Reverend Phelps scrutinized the congregation. "Good morning. I'm glad to see so many bright faces."

An elderly lady in the front row raised both hands. "Amen."

He shuffled his notes. "Today I'd like to talk about the need to respect our bodies—the temples we have been granted during our short sojourn on Earth."

A collective groan rolled through the crowd. Every sermon for three weeks had been about the perils of drugs and strong drink. Somewhere near the back of the church, a snore rumbled.

The Reverend thumped his fist on the pulpit. "Today's sermon will be about the necessity of sufficient sleep. I am disappointed at the number of my parishioners who snooze during church."

Notes: All dialogue tags and extraneous action beats have been eliminated. There is no need to say that the old lady raised her hands *in the air.*

Every night, I must say, and *every Sunday* were removed to streamline the dialogue and make it more natural.

Several verbs were replaced by stronger equivalents:

looked at = *scrutinized*

went = *rolled*

sounded = *rumbled*

hit = *thumped*

Adverb Abuse

Are you excited by your writing?

Mark Twain once said "I am dead to adverbs; they cannot excite me." If your writing shouts *lackluster,* an overabundance of adverbs might be the problem.

Consider the definition of *adverb:* any word or phrase that modifies a verb, adjective, or adverb.

Search your WIP for all words ending in *-ly.* Most will be adverbs. Although *–ly* words aren't the only culprits, replacing them when possible will tighten your writing.

The following guidelines will help.

Choose stronger verbs.

Which of the following sentences do you prefer?

Harold moved softly toward the door.

Harold walked softly toward the door.

Harold tiptoed toward the door.

A strong verb in the third example removes the necessity for an *-ly* adverb, thereby decreasing word count and painting a better scene in readers' minds.

Evaluate the following phrases and their suggested replacements.

Appear gradually: emerge, fade in, materialize

Ascend quickly: skyrocket, soar, spring

Ask sleepily: mumble, murmur, mutter

Break violently: burst, explode, rupture

Breathe heavily: gasp, pant, wheeze

Burn brightly: blaze, flare, glare

Change slightly: acclimate, adapt, adjust

Check continuously: monitor, surveil, watch

Chew continuously: chomp, gnaw, munch

Close loudly: bang, slam

Collide violently: crash, plow into, slam into

Destroy utterly: annihilate, decimate, extirpate, obliterate

Drink greedily: devour, guzzle, swill

Eat hurriedly: bolt, gobble, inhale

Enfold clumsily: clinch, grope, manhandle

Examine closely: analyze, inspect, scrutinize

Fall suddenly: plummet, plunge, nosedive

Flicker intermittently: fluctuate, gutter, twinkle

Flow rapidly: gush, spout, surge

Flow slowly: dribble, drip, seep, trickle

Follow carefully: shadow, track, trail

Grab clumsily: fumble, grope, scrabble

Hold gently: cradle, cuddle, cushion

Hush obstinately: choke, clam up, stifle

Investigate fully: analyze, reconnoiter, scrutinize

Knock noisily: beat, hammer, pound

Laugh hugely: bellow, guffaw, roar

Look curiously: contemplate, examine, study

Look nearsightedly: peer, squinch, squint

Look quietly: glance, peek, regard

Look steadfastly: gaze, goggle, stare

Miss frightfully: ache for, pine for, yearn for

Move cautiously: prowl, pussyfoot, slink

Move convulsively: convulse, judder, spasm

Move quickly: catapult, gallop, hurtle

Move slightly: edge, stir, twitch

Nod gloomily: droop, shrug, slouch

Object strongly: condemn, oppose, protest

Poke experimentally: examine, probe, prod

React grimly: caution, forewarn, lour

React irritably: glower, grumble, threaten

Repair temporarily: improvise, jury-rig, make do

Retreat hastily: abscond, escape, flee

Rub vigorously: burnish, scour, scrub

Run quickly: dart, race, sprint

Sink ponderously: collapse, drop, plunge

Smell potently: pong, reek, stink

Smile foolishly: simper, smirk, snicker

Smile pleasantly: beam, glow, grin

Speak abruptly: retort, snap, snarl

Speak bitterly: complain, grouse, grumble

Speak excitedly: exclaim, rant, vociferate

Speak feebly: snivel, whimper, whine

Speak grumpily: complain, grumble, grump

Speak hesitantly: dither, hedge, vacillate

Speak loudly: bellow, roar, thunder

Speak meditatively: posit, postulate, theorize

Speak quietly: mumble, murmur, whisper

Speak suddenly: blurt, interject, interrupt

Spit disgustedly: deride, gob, hawk

Stand solemnly: brood, meditate; mourn

Step gingerly: creep, pad, tiptoe

Strike violently: assault, clobber, punch

Suggest eagerly: advocate, insist, urge

Take seriously: accept, acknowledge, believe

Talk longwindedly: blather, drone, prattle

Tap nervously: drum, fidget, wriggle

Throb painfully: ache, pound, twinge

Touch gingerly: brush, pat, tap

Tread heavily: slog, tramp, trudge

Trip repeatedly: stagger, stumble, totter

Try desperately: labor, strive, struggle

Wade energetically: slosh, splash, sploosh

Walk gracefully: glide, float, slink

Walk painfully: hobble, limp, lurch

Walk slowly: amble, saunter, stroll

Walk softly: creep, sneak, tiptoe

Walk tiredly: clod, lumber, plod

Want badly: covet, crave, need

Watch helplessly: cringe, despair, flounder

Wind slowly: meander, snake, twist

Analyze adverbs of degree.

Rather than strengthen narrative, qualifiers often weaken it. The following list includes a few -*ly* adverbs of degree collected from books I've read. In many cases instead of replacing a phrase, the adverb could be omitted.

Abnormally grumpy: cantankerous, churlish, crabby

Absolutely afraid: horrified, petrified, terrified

Absolutely outstanding: exceptional, stupendous, superior

Amazingly fierce: ferocious, savage, vicious

Appallingly bad: abysmal, appalling, terrible

Astonishingly harsh: abrasive, caustic, rough

Awesomely powerful: almighty, invincible, omnipotent

Awfully dirty: filthy, grimy, soiled

Brightly clad: gaudy, ostentatious, showy

Cautiously optimistic: encouraged, hopeful, upbeat

Considerably large: huge, humongous, massive

Deeply channeled: furrowed, grooved, rutted

Deliberately inappropriate: facetious, flippant, sardonic

Desperately cold: freezing, icy, wintry

Distressingly hungry: famished, ravenous, starving

Dreadfully tired: drained, exhausted, spent

Enormously creepy: frightening, macabre, sinister

Especially charming: captivating, endearing, prepossessing

Exceedingly happy: delighted, ecstatic, thrilled

Exceptionally good: fantastic, outstanding, superb

Excessively small: diminutive, miniscule, tiny

Extraordinarily eager: ardent, impatient, keen

Extremely glossy: brilliant, dazzling, glaring

Extremely important: crucial, imperative, vital

Genuinely funny: hilarious, sidesplitting, uproarious

Ghastly pale: ashen, pallid, wan

Hopelessly dependent: helpless, incapable, vulnerable

Horribly frightened: horrified, petrified, terrified

Incredibly old: ancient, hoary, timeworn

Indescribably unpleasant: hideous, repulsive, revolting

Intensely preoccupied: absorbed, engrossed, fascinated

Markedly doubtful: cynical, skeptical, unconvinced

Noticeably depressed: gloomy, glum, melancholy

Overly brazen: arrogant, brash, insolent

Overpoweringly noisy: deafening, roaring, thunderous

Overwhelmingly tasty: delectable, delicious, scrumptious

Particularly calm: placid, serene, tranquil

Pleasantly melodic: dulcet, musical, tuneful

Profoundly dark: black, Stygian, unlit

Really hot: blistering, boiling, torrid

Remarkably careful: cautious, vigilant, wary

Richly carved: elaborate, ornate, sculpted

Seriously wrong: calamitous, dire, disastrous

Severely cruel: brutal, inhumane, savage

Slightly wet: clammy, damp, moist

Strikingly beautiful: gorgeous, striking, stunning

Strongly resistant: defiant, obstinate, uncooperative

Superbly gifted: accomplished, adept, talented

Terribly anxious: apprehensive, overwrought, perturbed

Totally amazing: astonishing, astounding, mind-boggling

Tremendously courageous: bold, fearless, undaunted

Truly ugly: hideous, repulsive, revolting

Unbelievably healthy: hardy, robust, vigorous

Universally accepted: familiar, known, recognized

Unusually awkward: clumsy, inept, uncoordinated

Utterly ashamed: disgraced, humiliated, mortified

Additional adverbs of degree include *almost, enough, just, most, much, quite, rather, somewhat, too, very*, et al.

Remove redundant adverbs that modify adjectives.

Many modified adjectives fly better solo. If a comment is negative, do you need to describe it as *purely negative?* Analyze every adverb-adjective pair. Many adjectives are absolute and should never be modified.

Here are a few phrases to get you started.

Absolutely catastrophic: catastrophic

Absolutely stunned: stunned

Absolutely critical: critical

Absolutely defeated: defeated

Apparently uninjured: uninjured

Badly broken: broken

Completely blank: blank

Completely harmless: harmless

Completely poisoned: poisoned

Directly ahead: ahead

Entirely unmarked: unmarked

Exactly sure: sure

Fully charged: charged

Particularly acute: acute

Perfectly balanced: balanced

Perfectly right: right

Perfectly willing: willing

Purely negative: negative

Seriously alarmed: alarmed

Thoroughly honest: honest

Totally absorbent: absorbent

Totally insane: insane

Totally unexpected: unexpected

Utterly desolate: desolate

Utterly devastated: devastated

Utterly foolish: foolish

Utterly motionless: motionless

Visibly distressed: distressed

Remove redundant adverbs that modify verbs.

Review the following phrases. If you check the definitions of the verbs, you'll see why the modifying adverbs are superfluous.

Caress lovingly: caress

Chastise severely: chastise

Crush forcefully: crush

Dwindle gradually: dwindle

Jab roughly: jab

Lap softly: lap

Pad noiselessly: pad

Plummet rapidly: plummet

Relish greatly: relish

Slurp noisily: slurp

Smack sharply: smack

Suddenly notice: notice

… and so on. Whenever you see an adverb-verb combination, proceed with caution.

Beware. Some –*ly* words are adjectives.

If an -*ly* word modifies a noun or a pronoun, it's an adjective:

The teenager's voice was crackly.
The teenager had a crackly voice.

The blow he delivered was deadly.
He delivered a deadly blow.

Her personality seemed friendly.
She seemed to have a friendly personality.

His scent was manly.
He had a manly scent.

The bumps covering his arms looked ungainly.
Ungainly bumps covered his arms.

Delete *suddenly*.

The *suddenly* trap snares many writers. Ditto for *abruptly, unexpectedly, precipitously,* etc.

For instance:

Wanda moved into the backyard. Suddenly she heard a loud noise behind her. She turned toward it.

Study this edited version:

Wanda crept into the backyard. A growl rumbled behind her. She whipped around.

Note the subtle changes and strong verbs in the second passage. With four fewer words, including deletion of *suddenly*, we see a more vivid picture.

If you require sudden action, and you've already repeated *suddenly* too often, investigate alternatives such as:

All at once

All of a sudden

At once

At that moment

Forthwith

From nowhere

In a flash

In an instant

Just then

Straightaway

With precipitous speed

Without delay

Without hesitation

Without notice

Without warning

Ready to exercise your adverb acumen?

Remove all -*ly* adverbs in the following:

Exercise 1

The softly burbling stream wound slowly through the forest, gently lapping at brightly glistening rocks. Kelly waded carefully into the water and sighed contentedly.

Suggested solution

The burbling stream meandered through the forest, lapping at glistening rocks. Kelly slipped into the water. "Ahhhhh," she murmured.

Notes: Strong verbs tighten the narrative. There is no need to modify *glistening*. Dialogue *shows* Kelly's contented sigh.

Exercise 2

Anxiously, I walked over the slowly swaying footbridge, desperately wrestling with the horribly overpowering nausea that suddenly threatened my hopelessly knotted stomach. My poorly secured backpack flopped rudely with every nervously placed step. My exhalations wheezed inexorably, filling the mysteriously dark air with rapidly swirling spirals of steam.

Soon, an icily cold blanket of clamminess enveloped me in its wildly tight embrace. Twisting tendrils—writhingly probing through the malodorous ether—enfolded me even more tightly and tenaciously than the grotesquely intimate caress of the dampness. They pushed on my chest, hungrily, insistently, forcefully ...

I awoke and felt about blindly for my asthma inhaler.

Suggested solution

I tiptoed over the swaying footbridge as I wrestled overwhelming nausea, my backpack flopping with every movement. My anxious wheezing filled the dark air with swirling steam spirals. An icy blanket of clamminess enveloped me in its tight embrace. Twisting tendrils writhed through the malodorous ether and enfolded me in their tenacious grip. They crushed my chest ...

I awoke and groped for my asthma inhaler.

Notes: Most sources discourage opening with a dream, although this snippet could work if presented as part of an ongoing medical condition. Strong verbs and adjectives eliminate the necessity for adverbs. There's no need to describe the backpack as *poorly secured;* its flopping *shows* that. *Soon,* like *suddenly,* can often be eliminated.

Alright

Is *alright* ever alright?

According to EtymOnline.com, *alright* was attested in print by 1884.

Writers argue about its use. Some insist it's appropriate, while others stand on the *no-nada-nix-never* soapbox.

Who is correct? This chapter will attempt to allay the confusion.

What do the experts say about *alright*?

I searched several sources and found the following results.

<u>1. No, it is unacceptable:</u>

Painless Grammar by Rebecca Elliott, PhD

The Chicago Manual of Style

AP Stylebook

Lapsing into a Comma by Bill Walsh

<u>2. It doesn't even appear in these reference books:</u>

The Synonym Finder by J. I. Rodale

Elements of Style by William Strunk Jr.

<u>3. It is informal and nonstandard.</u>

Dictionary.com

Merriam-Webster.com

Dictionary.Cambridge.org

OxfordDictionaries.com

MacMillanDictionary.com

YourDictionary.com

CollinsDictionary.com

TheFreeDictionary.com

4. Ray Bradbury's style reinforces point 1.

My hunt through several Ray Bradbury e-books found no instances of *alright*.

5. Other pundits agree.

After more research, I couldn't locate a single source that championed the word.

Does that mean writers should avoid it?

Maybe.

But everything is acceptable in dialogue, right?

Wrong.

Do you see speech balloons when you have a conversation with someone? You can't determine whether a person is saying *there, their,* or *they're; alright, all-right,* or *all right.*

Readers will judge written dialogue the same way they do narrative.

Let's review a few examples.

Group 1

"Alright, I'll go," Sherri said.

"Okay, I'll go," Sherri said.

In context, we understand that Sherri, if not happy, is at least willing to go. However, details are sketchy. Readers should know how she is feeling. We can *show* her emotions with a few details:

Sherri stamped one foot and glared at me. "Fine! I'll go."

Readers will now see a belligerent Sherri.

Sherri's eyes sparkled. "Sure, I'll go."

This Sherri is happy.

Even though Trystan's clay sculpture resembled a blob more than a ballerina, ~~he knew~~ the teacher would tell him it was <u>alright</u>.

Even though Trystan's clay sculpture resembled a blob more than a ballerina, ~~he knew~~ the teacher would tell him it was <u>good enough</u>.

Note the strikeout of *he knew*. This is written from Trystan's point of view. Of course, he knows. Stating so is redundant and distracting.

Why would a teacher inform Trystan that his mediocre work is acceptable?

Miss Proctor sidled up to Trystan and whispered in his ear, "Come to my place tonight, and I'll give you a passing grade for that sloppy sculpture."

Will Trystan accept Miss Proctor's offer?

Trystan gazed at his lopsided clay sculpture and texted his teacher: "Remember. Passing grade or I release the photos."

Two contrasting scenarios grow from the same idea.

A case could be made for avoiding both *alright* and *all right*.

When submitting your writing to contests or literary journals, you're unlikely to know the preferences of judges and editors. If you're writing a book, your readers will be split between the *alright* and *all right* supporters.

Nervous?

After reading this information, you might hesitate before using either form. Bearing that in mind, I located alternatives, including several clichés that would be suitable for dialogue.

More than 100 *alright/all right* alternatives:

A
A-OK, above-board, absolutely, acceptable, adequate, agreed, appropriate, average

B
Banal, bearable, below-standard, boring, by all means

C
Certainly, *comme ci, comme ça*, commonplace, copacetic, corny

D
Decent, doable, drab, dreary, dull

E
Effective, everyday

F
Fair, fair-to-middling, feasible, fine, fit, fitting

G
Good, good enough

H
Hackneyed, humdrum, hunky-dory

I
Indeed, indifferent, insipid

J
Jake

K
Kosher

L
Legit, legitimate

M
Mediocre, meet, middle-of-the-road, middling, monotonous, mundane

N
Nice, no great shakes, no problem, not bad, not too bad, nothing special, nothing to write home about

O
Of course, OK, okay, okeydokey, ordinary

P
Passable, pedestrian, permissible, pleasing, predictable, presentable, pretty good, proper

R
Reasonable, respectable, right-o, routine, run-of-the-mill

S
Satisfactory, second-class, second-rate, seemly, so-so, sound, stale, straight up, sufficient, suitable, sure, swell

T
Tacky, tasteless, tawdry, tedious, tenable, tired, tiresome, tolerable, trite, typical

U
Undistinguished, unexceptional, unexciting, unimaginative, uninspired, unoriginal, unremarkable, unsurprising, up to scratch, up to standard

V
Vapid, viable

W
Whatever, whatever you say, within acceptable limits, workable, worn-out

Y
Yeah, yep, yes, you bet

Exercises and story prompts:

Revise the following passages to eliminate *alright*.

Exercise 1

Even though the wailing of police sirens grew louder every heartbeat, Anton knew everything would be <u>alright</u>.

Of course it'll be <u>alright</u>. I don't have any on me ... "Damn!"

[Why does Anton curse? What could he be carrying that might incriminate him? Can you turn this into a funny story? A horror flash, perhaps?]

Exercise 2

Gabriel slumped to the floor, eyes unfocussed, and froth bubbling from between his lips.

"Are you <u>alright</u>?" I asked.

His body convulsed, contorting him into a shape that should have been impossible for anyone without double joints.

Of course he wasn't <u>alright</u>, and it was my fault. Why hadn't I _____?

Exercise 3

To say Anja's performance was <u>alright</u> would mislead my audience. It's <u>alright</u> being a Broadway critic, but some days I'm at a loss for words when I encounter an actress like Anja Mehler.

[What will this critic say next? Was Anja's performance good or bad? In this instance, it's unclear—an excellent reason to avoid *alright*. The phrasing of the first sentence could lead to either a flattering or a dismal review.]

Exercise 4

Never in a million years could Petra have expected anything like what she saw next.

<u>Alright</u>. It's going to be <u>alright</u>.

Cold sweat turned her T-shirt into a sopping dishrag within seconds. But that dishrag didn't alleviate the sweltering heat rising through the vents in the floor.

Her gaze shifted to a translucent shape shimmering between her and her only escape—a security door protected by an alphanumeric keypad.

Twelve characters. Millions of possibilities. Maybe billions.

It's not going to be alright. I shoulda known better. How in blazes am I gonna get myself out of this one?

[Petra could be a thief attempting to burgle something. But what is the translucent shape? She might be on a spaceship, struggling to reach the helm or airlock. Or this could be a setup for steampunk sci-fi.]

Ambiguous Verbs

Ambiguous verbs weaken writing.

Which of these sentences prompts a more powerful image?

He walked to the door.

He plodded to the door.

The second example *shows* readers a character who might be tired, lonely, or depressed. One verb paints a powerful picture.

Some sources advocate *show* almost to the exclusion of *tell*. A frequent consequence of this approach is word bloat. However, well-chosen verbs deliver precise meanings. They invigorate writing without increasing word count.

Harness strong verbs and their diverse nuances.

The child was under her guardian's care.

This statement offers one basic fact but no details that might further the story.

Review the following three revisions. Each replaces *was* with a stronger alternative:

The child thrived under her guardian's care.

This child is healthy. We intuit a caring guardian who probably feeds her well and attends to her physical and emotional needs.

The child endured under her guardian's care.

The second child might be alive in spite of her guardian's care. Perhaps he abuses her physically or emotionally.

The child subsisted under her guardian's care.

The third child survives, albeit at a minimal level. Perhaps the guardian doesn't provide a healthy diet or clean environment.

Evaluate another scenario:

Alyssa walked toward the table while she looked at the grandfather clock next to the china cabinet. The clock chimed midnight. She pulled out her phone and touched the screen. Three hours. Henry had been gone for three hours.

We see a woman who is waiting for Henry. However, we don't know whether she's worried or angry. Let's change the underlined verbs:

Alyssa trudged toward the table while she stared at the grandfather clock next to the china cabinet. The clock chimed midnight. She dragged out her phone and fondled the screen. Three hours. Henry had been gone for three hours.

The strong verbs *show* an Alyssa who seems worried, perhaps even depressed. She fondles the screen of her phone. Maybe her screensaver is a photo of Henry.

Alyssa stomped toward the table while she glared at the grandfather clock next to the china cabinet. The clock chimed midnight. She jerked out her phone and jabbed the screen. Three hours. Henry had been gone for three hours.

Do you have any doubt that this Alyssa is angry?

A final set of examples:

Sparks appeared in the hallway, and smoke blew into the coffee room. Trent went to the fire alarm and pulled the handle. He listened. No sound from the alarm. He moved toward the emergency exit.

In view of the circumstances, Trent seems illogically nonchalant.

Sparks erupted in the hallway, and smoke billowed into the coffee room. Trent raced to the fire alarm and wrenched the handle. He concentrated. No sound from the alarm. He inched toward the emergency exit.

This Trent acts suitably anxious, but he exhibits care while he moves through the smoke toward the emergency exit.

The cheat sheet:

The following list contains several common verbs, along with suggested alternatives.

Appear: emerge, erupt, expand, flash into view, materialize, pop up, solidify, spread out, surface, take shape, unfold, unfurl, unwrap

Be: bloom, blossom, endure, exist, flourish, last, live, manage, persevere, persist, prevail, remain, stay, subsist, survive, thrive

Begin: activate, commence, create, initiate, launch, originate [Do you need *begin, start,* or their relatives? Writing is usually stronger without them.]

Believe: accept, admit, affirm, conjecture, hope, hypothesize, imagine, postulate, presume, speculate, surmise, suspect, trust

Blow: billow, blast, curl, drift, eddy, flow, flutter, fly, gasp, glide, gust, puff, roar, sail, scud, sough, storm, surge, swell, undulate, waft, whirl

Break: crush, decimate, demolish, destroy, disintegrate, flatten, fracture, fragment, raze, shatter, smash, snap, splinter, split

Bring: bear, carry, cart, drag, draggle, ferry, fetch, forward, haul, heave, heft, lug, relay, schlep, send, shuttle, tow, transport

Close: bang shut, bar, block, blockade, bolt, bung, cork, fasten, latch, lock, obstruct, plug, seal, secure, slam, squeeze shut, stopper

Come: advance, approach, arrive, draw near, drive, enter, fly, near, proceed, reach, show up, slip in, sneak, travel, turn up

Cry: bawl, bellow, bleat, blubber, howl, keen, mewl, moan, snivel, scream, sob, squall, squeal, wail, weep, whimper, whine, yelp

Disappear: atomize, crumble, disband, disperse, dissipate, dissolve, evaporate, fade away, fizzle out, melt away, scatter, vaporize

Do: accomplish, achieve, attempt, complete, consummate, enact, execute, fulfill, implement, perform, shoulder, undertake

Eat: bolt, chomp, consume, devour, dine, gobble, gnaw at, gorge, guzzle, ingest, inhale, munch, nibble, pick at, scarf, wolf down

Feel (1): appreciate, bear, encounter, endure, experience, face, tolerate, stand, suffer, suspect, undergo, weather, withstand

Feel (2): brush, caress, finger, fondle, grope, knead, manipulate, massage, palpate, pat, paw, poke, press, prod, rub, stroke, tap

Get: annex, acquire, appropriate, attain, capture, clear, collect, earn, gain, gather, gross, land, procure, purchase, score, secure, steal, win

Give: award, bequeath, bestow, confer, contribute, deliver, donate, grant, lend, offer, present, proffer, turn over, volunteer, vouchsafe

Go: abscond, bolt, escape, exit, flee, fly, hightail it, journey, retire, retreat, sally, scram, set out, split, travel, vamoose, withdraw

Have: boast, brandish, conserve, control, display, enjoy, flaunt, hoard, husband, keep, maintain, own, possess, preserve, retain

Help: abet, aid, alleviate, assist, augment, back, bolster, comfort, encourage, improve, relieve, rescue, sanction, succor, support

Hold: capture, clasp, clench, cling, clutch, cuddle, embrace, enfold, envelop, grapple, grasp, grip, hug, pinch, seize, snatch, squeeze

Jump: bob, bobble, bounce, bound, caper, cavort, clear, frisk, hop, hurdle, jolt, jounce, leap, leapfrog, rocket, romp, skip, spring, vault

Know: appreciate, comprehend, fathom, follow, grasp, identify, perceive, realize, recollect, recognize, register, twig, understand

Let: accept, acquiesce, allow, approve, authorize, consent, empower, enable, facilitate, license, okay, permit, sanction, suffer, tolerate

Like: admire, adore, adulate, cherish, dote, enjoy, esteem, honor, idolize, relish, respect, revere, savor, treasure, venerate, worship

Listen: earwig, concentrate, eavesdrop, focus on, heed, monitor, overhear, pay attention, perk the ears, snoop, spy, take note

Look: eye, examine, gape, gawk, gaze, glance, glare, goggle, inspect, ogle, peek, peer, rubberneck, scrutinize, stare, study, survey

Move: advance, budge, climb, creep, edge, gallivant, inch, progress, reposition, shift, sidle, slide, slink, slip, slither, stir, tiptoe, travel

Occur: arise, befall, betide, chance, coalesce, crop up, crystalize, ensue, eventuate, manifest, supervene, surface, transpire

Pull: drag, draw, extract, haul, jerk, lug, mine, pluck, schlep, seize, snatch, tow, trawl, troll, tug, tweak, twist, withdraw, wrench, yank

Put: arrange, deposit, drop, dump, lay, leave, lodge, organize, park, place, plant, plonk, plunk, position, push, release, stash, wedge

Run: bolt, charge, dart, dash, gallop, hurtle, jog, lope, race, rush, scamper, scurry, scoot, shoot, speed, sprint, tear, trot, zip, zoom

See: detect, differentiate, discover, distinguish, glimpse, identify, notice, observe, perceive, recognize, sight, spot, view, witness

Shake: agitate, churn, convulse, jiggle, joggle, jostle, judder, quake, quiver, rock, seethe, shudder, sway, tremble, vibrate, wobble

Sit: alight, collapse into, drop into, fall into, flop, hang, loll, lounge, park, perch, recline, rest, roost, settle, slump into, sprawl, straddle

Smile: beam, brighten, dimple, flash the teeth, glow, grin, leer, light up, radiate delight, simper, smirk, sneer, snigger, sparkle, twinkle

Speak: articulate, chat, chatter, converse, enunciate, gossip, mumble, murmur, natter, orate, parley, proclaim, verbalize, vocalize, whisper

Take: carry, cart, conduct, convey, deliver, escort, ferry, guide, marshal, shepherd, shoulder, steer, tote, transfer, transport, usher

Talk: argue, blather, burble, confer, converse, debate, deliberate, discuss, lecture, maunder, prate, splutter, sputter, stammer, stutter

Tell: announce, apprise, assert, avow, chronicle, claim, declare, describe, disclose, divulge, maintain, narrate, proclaim, report, reveal

Think: conceive, concoct, contemplate, deliberate, dream, envisage, imagine, invent, meditate, muse, ponder, reflect, visualize, weigh

Touch: caress, elbow, finger, fondle, graze, handle, jab, jostle, manhandle, mess, pat, scrape, scratch, shove, stroke, tap, tousle

Turn: circle, gyrate, gyre, pirouette, pivot, reel, revolve, rotate, spin, spiral, swivel, twirl, twist, twizzle, wheel, whip around, whirl

Understand: absorb, believe, cognize, comprehend, conclude, decipher, fathom, grasp, interpret, make out, make sense of, unravel

Use: apply, channel, deploy, employ, establish, exercise, exploit, harness, maneuver, manipulate, practice, ply, utilize, wield

Walk: amble, dance, drift, march, meander, parade, patrol, plod, promenade, saunter, slog, stomp, stroll, trek, tromp, trudge, wander

Watch: eyeball, follow, guard, inspect, observe, police, protect, safeguard, scan, scrutinize, stalk, study, surveil, survey, track, view

Work: aspire, drudge, endeavor, exert oneself, fight, grind, labor, slog, skivvy, strain, strive, struggle, sweat, toil, travail, wrestle

Ready for a few verb calisthenics?

Replace the underlined words with stronger choices.

Exercise 1

With a scowl on her face, Endora put her arms across her chest and looked at Samantha. "You haven't looked like that since your father won the Mr. Universe Pageant two centuries ago. What's up?"

"Oh, nothing." Samantha smiled. "Darrin just received a promotion, and we're going to the Bahamas to celebrate."

"Goodie. I can babysit while you're gone."

"Sorry, Mom. The kids are going with us."

A thunderclap sounded. The house shook. Endora looked at her daughter. "They're what?"

Endora <u>crossed her arms</u> and <u>scowled</u> at Samantha. "You haven't looked like that since your father won the Mr. Universe Pageant two centuries ago. What's up?"

"Oh, nothing." Samantha <u>grinned</u>. "Darrin just received a promotion, and we're going to the Bahamas to celebrate."

"Goodie. I can babysit while you're gone."

"Sorry, Mom. The kids are going with us."

A thunderclap <u>boomed</u>. The house <u>juddered</u>. Endora <u>glared</u> at her daughter. "They're what?"

Notes: Put her arms across her chest becomes *crossed her arms*. Dialogue remains as is to seem realistic, including Samantha's repetition of *going*. The short sentences in the final paragraph speed the action and amplify the tension.

Exercise 2

What's that noise? Angela <u>turned</u> around. She <u>listened</u>.

Maximus <u>appeared</u> in the mist. She <u>moved</u> toward him—close, closer. She <u>touched</u> his arm. He <u>spoke</u> so quietly she couldn't <u>understand</u> his words.

Puzzled, she <u>looked</u> into his eyes. He <u>looked</u> back with opaque amber orbs.

She <u>shook</u>.

Suggested solution

What's that noise? Angela <u>whipped</u> around. She <u>concentrated</u>.

Maximus <u>materialized</u> in the mist. She <u>inched</u> toward him—close, closer—and <u>caressed</u> his arm. He <u>mumbled</u> so quietly she couldn't <u>decipher</u> his words.

Puzzled, she <u>peered</u> into his eyes. He <u>stared</u> back with opaque amber orbs.

She <u>trembled</u>.

Notes: Each verb in the suggested solution was selected from the cheat sheet.

Exercise 3

Timmy put his tooth under his pillow and smiled at Mummy. "When will the Tooth Fairy come?"

She touched his forehead. "Not until you're asleep. When she hears you snoring, she'll sneak in. You'll never see her, because she makes herself invisible."

He closed his eyes and made a snoring noise.

Mummy touched his hair. "Nuh-uh. She's too smart to fall for that."

"Awwww. But I want to see her."

Suggested solution

Timmy stashed his tooth under his pillow and beamed at Mummy. "When will the Tooth Fairy come?"

She stroked his forehead. "Not until you're asleep. When she hears you snoring, she'll sneak in. You'll never see her, because she makes herself invisible."

He squeezed his eyes shut and faked a snore.

Mummy tousled his hair. "Nuh-uh. She's too smart to fall for that."

"Awwww. But I want to see her."

Notes: Once again, dialogue is untouched. The replacements are straightforward.

Crutch Words

Crutch words: insidious creepers.

They camouflage as benign buds, but these malignant weeds propagate throughout your work and choke its vitality.

This chapter will cover a few of the most frequent offenders: a lot, actually, all, almost, anyway, apparently, basically, definitely, especially, essentially, even, honestly, just, like, literally, obviously, only, quite, really, seriously, simply, so, something, very, and truly.

During the revision process, ask five important questions:

1. Do the crutch words advance narrative?

2. Can you find more specific words?

3. Can you make a generalization specific?

4. Is it possible to *show* instead of *tell*?

5. Would specificity solve the problem?

The fastest fix is deletion.

Crutch words contribute nothing more than fluff. Rather than complement writing, they diminish its impact. Delete them. Then read your work out loud to see if it conveys the desired effect. If not, create alternatives.

Practical application:

The following sections offer examples of crutch-word elimination. Exploit them as idea starters.

<u>A lot</u>

He looks a lot like his brother.
He resembles his brother.

She likes him a lot.
She has a crush on him.

They have a lot in common.
They share similar interests.

Actually

He didn't actually say he liked her.
He didn't admit he liked her.

She actually saw his six-pack.
She gawked at his six-pack.

He actually said he needs a loan.
He said he needs $1000.

All

All the children recited the poem.
The fifth-grade class recited the poem.

All the research contradicts that.
Comprehensive research contradicts that.

All of them went to the fair.
The family went to the fair.

Almost

Almost twenty people showed up.
Nineteen people showed up.

I'm almost sure he left already.
I think he left already.

She almost vomited.
Nausea overcame her.

Anyway

He decided to try it anyway.
He decided to attempt it.

Anyway, it didn't taste too bad.
The taste was acceptable.

Anyway, it costs too much.
It's too expensive.

Apparently

Apparently, he's married.
He has a wife and three kids.

Her answer was apparently ironic.
Her ironic answer made everyone laugh.

The motor apparently died.
The motor seized and refused to restart.

Basically

He's basically too old for the marathon.
His arthritis won't allow him to run in the marathon.

She basically answered the test question correctly.
She misspelled her answer, which resulted in a loss of one mark on the test.

Basically, he was on his own.
Both parents disappeared when he was sixteen, leaving him to fend for himself.

Definitely

She's definitely not interested.
She's unapproachable.

This car is definitely old.
This car is an antique.

They definitely disagreed.
They quarreled.

Especially

It gets hot here, especially at night.
Days here are hot. Nights are sweltering.

I was especially interested in the Yorkie.
I had to have that Yorkie.

We need a break, especially Curtis.
Curtis needs a break. We do too.

Essentially

The process is essentially automatic.
The process requires little intervention.

Essentially, he owns two mansions.
Although he owns two mansions, they are over-mortgaged.

Newborns essentially sleep most of the day.
Newborns sleep sixteen to seventeen hours a day.

Even

Even a dolt could understand this.
Anyone could understand this.

Not even two hours passed before he woke again.
Fewer than two hours passed before he woke again.

She hadn't even been to Egypt yet but was in love with it.
She couldn't wait for her first trip to Egypt.

Honestly

Honestly, this is the hardest thing I've ever had to do.
This is the most difficult problem I've ever encountered.

I can honestly say I forgot.
Sorry, I forgot.

It was honestly the best pizza I ever ate.
The pizza tasted scrumptious—the best I ever ate.

Just

He was just a little too old for the competition.
The competition cut-off was nineteen years of age, but he was twenty.

It's not just the teachers who disagree with the changes.
Teachers—and parents—disagree with the changes.

No matter what Mom did, the baby's fever just kept getting worse.
The baby's fever worsened no matter what Mom did.

Like

He looked like a cat ready to pounce.
He resembled a cat ready to pounce.

Like her mother, she detested the smell of garlic.
She and her mother detested the smell of garlic.

He acted like an uptight despot.
He demanded unconditional loyalty.

Literally

She was literally broke.
Her bank account was as empty as her gas tank.

His basement, literally overflowing with water, smelled of mold and dead rats.
His flooded basement reeked of mold and dead rats.

Her observations were literally true.
Her observations were flawless.

Obviously

He was obviously embarrassed.
He bit his lip and shifted in his seat. Then his face turned red.

She stared at him, obviously confused.
She frowned at him while she fumbled with her phone.

He obviously detested her enthusiasm.
Whenever she made an enthusiastic remark, he bared his teeth.

Only

She owned only a few pairs of shoes.
She owned sneakers, flats, and a pair of heels with a broken strap.

His only regret was never having married.
His greatest regrets were never having had a wife to confide in, never fathering children, never having a family dog to greet him at the door.

Her actions only made the situation worse.
Her machinations exacerbated the situation.

Quite

He was quite smitten by the woman.
Whenever the woman came near, he grinned and stuttered.

Her jeans weren't quite large enough.
She struggled to pull on her jeans.

Quite a few hurricanes were expected this year.
More hurricanes than usual were expected this year.

Really

What really is the issue here is your attitude.
The issue here is your disgraceful attitude.

He really doesn't believe in the human impact on climate change.
He disbelieves that humans affect climate change.

She didn't really break the rules.
She bent the rules.

Seriously

He was seriously injured in the accident.
His accident caused life-threatening injuries.

She takes her role as oldest sister seriously.
She encourages and guides her younger siblings.

He spoke seriously.
His voice turned somber.

Simply

She simply clammed up.
She refused to speak.

If he had simply asked, she would have offered to help.
If he had requested, she would have volunteered.

She simply didn't have time to paint the mural.
She was too busy to paint the mural.

So

He spoke so loud that it hurt my ears.
His yelling hurt my ears.

She lived so far away from the store.
Bicycling wasn't an option for her eight-mile trip to the store.

The fog was so thick that it caused several accidents.
The dense fog triggered six accidents.

Something

He wanted something more than a peck on the cheek.
He yearned for a passionate kiss.

She mumbled something unintelligible, and then walked away.
She mumbled below her breath, and then stomped away.

He wanted something to eat. Now.
He needed food. Now.

He made a truly heroic effort to save the dog from being hit.
He made a superhuman effort to prevent the bulldog from being run over by a bus.

Her eyes flashed, truly evil and frightening.
Her eyes flashed, malevolent and terrifying.

He's a truly remarkable person.
He's an extraordinary humanitarian.

Very

She was very glad to see him.
Her face lit up with delight when she spotted him.

He is very protective of his desk.
His desk functions as his castle, defended by a deep glower whenever anyone dares to enter his cubicle and violate his "personal space."

She knew very little about the new boss.
The new boss was an enigma to her.

The simmer principle:

1. Edit your writing.

2. Allow it to simmer for as long as possible.

3. Appraise it.

4. Repeat the previous steps as many times as necessary.

5. Present your pièce de résistance to the world.

Feel

Which of the following is more engaging?

Dillan felt the sun burning his skin.

The relentless sun seared Dillan's exposed flesh.

Most people will prefer the second sentence.

If wording alienates editors, agents—and more importantly, readers—it poses a problem.

Feel isn't the culprit. Its overuse is.

Whenever you write about a character feeling something, you distance readers from the narrative. A better approach is to provide enough details for readers to experience what the character feels, without using *feel* or any of the alternatives in the list near the end of this chapter.

Let's review a few examples.

Example 1

The air was cold. Ethel <u>felt</u> it cutting through every crevice in her jacket.

Two faults stand out in the previous paragraph. *Was* produces a wishy-washy *tell*. The second sentence includes the filter word *felt*.

The frigid air cut through every crevice in Ethel's jacket. She shivered and pulled its faux-fur collar over her ears.

The edits provide a version that stimulates the senses.

Example 2

Roger <u>felt</u> dizzy as he stood on the edge of the cliff.

Pure *tell* again.

Roger picked his way to the edge of the cliff and peeked at the valley below. A gust of wind whipped his hair away from his face, and the world swam before his eyes. He staggered back a step.

Now we see a hesitant Roger, as demonstrated by *peeked*. The world swimming before his eyes *shows* his dizziness.

Example 3

David always _felt_ insecure around women.

Besides David's insecurity, we don't know anything about him. Let's add a few particulars:

Whenever David met a woman, he stared at his toes and couldn't remember any of his well-rehearsed come-ons.

This example evokes the image of an insecure man. The extra details *show* that David invests time creating smart lines, but when faced with reality, his insecurity wins out over preparation.

Example 4

A _feeling_ of sadness swept over Dwight as he gazed at Desiree's tombstone.

Although *feel* itself doesn't appear in this sentence, *a feeling of sadness* still distances readers.

We can expect a person to feel sad when viewing a tombstone, but the words don't provide any engagement.

Dwight fell to his knees before Desiree's tombstone and caressed the rough granite. Hot tears streamed down his cheeks.

Do you have any doubt that Dwight is sad? Having him fall to his knees rather than kneel amplifies the emotion. *Caress* embodies a gentle touch—associated with lovers—which is offset by the roughness of the granite. *Hot tears* adds a touch of temperature, and alludes to his relationship with Desiree.

Example 5

Will _felt_ a sharp pain in his side at mile five of the marathon, but he kept running.

This might work in flash fiction, but we could make it stronger:

At mile five of the marathon, Will clutched his side. Sharp spears of pain radiated through his body. Every breath became a labored gasp, but he kept running.

The extra information *shows* us a determined Will who doesn't intend to concede defeat.

Example 6

Quint felt the heat of embarrassment in his face. "Honest, I didn't mean to call you a witch," he said.

Although this example does arouse interest, we could increase its impact:

Quint pulled at his collar and winced. "Honest, I didn't mean to call you a witch," he stammered.

Quint's body language and stammering *show* his embarrassment.

Note the punctuation. *Winced*, part of an action beat, is followed by a period. You can't wince speech. Quint's words end with a comma, because *he stammered* could be replaced by *he said*, which is a dialogue tag.

Example 7

"I feel so lonely," Janelle said. "The house feels so empty now that Patrick is gone."

Anything a real person would say works in dialogue. However, the following sounds realistic too:

Janelle ran her fingers through her bedraggled hair. "I miss Patrick. Nobody to talk to. Nobody to share my bed. I cry myself to sleep every night."

Janelle's messy hair is one way of *showing* her loneliness. The amended dialogue does as well, without using a single instance of *feel*.

Base your judgment on the type of writing. Flash fiction will demand a concise approach. A novel allows more flexibility.

Example 8

Julie's mouth __felt__ dry while she waited for Scott.

Why? Maybe Julie is nervous:

Julie swallowed to moisten her dry mouth. The doorbell rang. She rushed toward the entrance. "Scott, is that you?"

Julie's actions *show* her nervousness, and enough information is provided to pique curiosity about Scott and her relationship with him.

Example 9

Bryan __felt__ sorry for the old homeless woman.

Rather than *tell* about Brian's sympathy, a few extra words could *show* it.

Bryan smiled at the old homeless woman and rummaged in his wallet for a bill. All he found was a parking ticket. He bit his lip. "Sorry, I don't have any cash on me. Can I buy you lunch?"

Bryan rummages for a bill, not a coin, and he doesn't give up when he can't find one—good insight into his character. His sympathy is more than token sentiment. The parking ticket could lead to an interesting side story.

Example 10

Bonnie __felt__ sure of her __feelings__ for Jens, but she didn't know how he __felt__ about her.

Teenage angst? This could be distilled into something more concise, or it could be expanded. Let's try a suitable approach for young-adult fiction:

Bonnie liked Jens. Did he like her back?

Or we could consider another possibility:

Whenever Bonnie was near Jens, she grinned like a demented cow and searched his eyes for any hint that he might return her affection.

The revised version might still work for YA, but it could also transition into adult romance.

Example 11

"I feel like an idiot," Martin said.

Real dialogue is often short and choppy:

"I'm an idiot," Martin said.

Rephrasing tightens the writing and reinforces Martin's opinion of himself.

Example 12

Charlene felt cold. Marc felt sorry for her. "Here," he said as he draped his jacket over her shoulders, "this should warm you up."

The previous paragraph demonstrates a couple of flaws.

Good writing deals with one point of view at a time. Switching POV, especially within the same paragraph, confuses readers.

Even without the POV problem, a new speaker should begin a new paragraph:

Charlene shivered.

Marc unbuttoned his jacket. "Here," he said as he draped it over her shoulders, "this should warm you up."

The changes eliminate *feel* filters and POV switching. Marc's action beat and dialogue appear in their own paragraph.

Example 13

Tammi felt terrified.

This example demonstrates pure *tell* with zero reader engagement.

Tammi cowered, wide-eyed, while she peered out of her hiding place. The burglar tiptoed close ... closer.

With a few edits, readers will now see Tammi's terror.

Alternatives for *feel:*

This list contains more than fifty alternatives for *feel*. However, many are filter words that detach readers from narrative. Choose with care, opting to *show* your characters' feelings whenever possible.

A
Abide, accept, allow, apperceive, appreciate, ascertain

B
Be aware of, be conscious of, be subjected to, bear, behold, brave, brook

C
Comprehend, conclude, confront, cope with, countenance

D
Deal with, descry, detect, determine, discern

E
Encounter, endure, enjoy, experience

F
Face

G
Get through, get vibes, go through, grasp

H
Have a hunch

I
Intuit

K
Know

L
Live through, live with

N
Notice

O
Observe

<u>P</u>
Perceive, put up with

<u>R</u>
Reconcile oneself to, remain, resign oneself to

<u>S</u>
Sense, spot, stand, stomach, submit to, succumb to, suffer, surrender to, survive, sustain

<u>T</u>
Take, tolerate

<u>U</u>
Undergo

<u>W</u>
Weather, withstand

<u>Y</u>
Yield to

Your turn.

Remove most forms of *feel* in the following exercises.

<u>Exercise 1</u>

Howard <u>felt</u> left out. Three months since the baby's birth, and he <u>felt</u> like a third thumb: useful for diaper changing, walking the floor with a shrieking infant, and bringing home his paycheck.

What about the good old days? Whenever he <u>felt</u> like a little loving and compassion from his wife, and she'd hop onto his lap?

He cracked a smile. Time to order flowers and reserve a table at Carol's favorite restaurant.

[What could go wrong? Is Howard heading for a huge disappointment? Maybe Carol isn't his wife.]

Exercise 2

Sandra <u>felt</u> sleepy. So sleepy. *I must stay awake. Just one more hour.* However, try as she might, her eyelids refused to cooperate, <u>feeling</u> heavier with every blink.

Just as she was about to slip into blessed oblivion, she <u>felt</u> the floor vibrate. Dust filled the air. She screamed.

[Is Sandra a captive? Why does she want to stay awake for just one more hour? Can you aim this in an unexpected direction?]

Exercise 3

Morgan <u>felt</u> soft kisses on his neck. Fingers caressed his chest. He opened his eyes and tried to focus in the dark. "Who are you, and what are you doing in my apartment?"

A warm mouth moved up to his lips ... and then to his ear. He <u>felt</u> a shiver as a quiet voice whispered, "I'm Victoria, and what you're going to <u>feel</u> next is recompense for what you did to my sister."

"Your sister?" Morgan made a fruitless attempt to move his arms. He <u>felt</u> something hard and plastic restraining his wrists. "Who's your sister?"

[This starts out sounding like every man's fantasy, but it quickly turns sour. Or does it? Could this lead to a funny story?]

Exercise 4

Erin <u>felt</u> betrayed. He had earned every nickel in the bank, every client, every contract. How dare his partner threaten him. He narrowed his eyes. A plan took shape—a plan that would empower him, make him <u>feel</u> like a magnate instead of a marionette.

He puffed out his chest and dialed the phone. It went to voice mail. *No matter.* "Hello, Clovis, you cretin. You won't get rid of me that easy. Two can play your game. Remember that girl you didn't want your wife to find out about? Guess who has a copy of your sex tape. Meet me. Mainstreet Deli. Noon. We'll discuss terms."

[How could Erin's plan fail? Does he really have the tape, or is he bluffing?]

"I don't <u>feel</u> like going to school today, Mom." Tim coughed and wiped his nose on his sleeve.

Edna <u>felt</u> his forehead. "You don't <u>feel</u> hot. Let me look in your mouth."

He stuck out his tongue.

"Your throat looks fine. Do you have a test today?"

Tim grimaced. "No ... _____"

[What would make a boy want to skip school? Bullies? A fight with a girlfriend? Something whacky and unexpected?]

Filter Words

This chapter provides a list of writing filters, with examples of how to replace them.

Although all words exist for a reason, filter words should be exploited sparingly to create the most engaging narrative.

Why should writers avoid filter words?

Because they act like a coffee machine.

Water takes time to drip through the filter while you wait for the reward: a delicious cup of aromatic ambrosia that glides down your throat.

Not a coffee drinker?

Recall the last time you stood in line at a bank or grocery store. You had to wait for service.

Wait.

That's what you force readers to do when you filter events through your characters' senses. Filter words form a barrier that distances readers from your story.

Study this example:

Bertie felt the warm sand between her toes as she walked.

Bertie's experience is relayed secondhand. When word economy is crucial, this approach works. However, wouldn't you rather become so involved that you almost feel it yourself?

With a few tweaks, we can strengthen the sentence:

The sand trickled between Bertie's toes, radiating warmth with every step she took.

Strong verbs, *trickled* and *radiating*, amplify the sensory impact.

Five senses? Six? Twelve?

Most people can name five senses: sight, smell, hearing, touch, and taste. Add ESP to the list, and it grows to six.

Some pundits expand to include pain, balance, motion, sense of time, temperature, and sense of direction. You might even discover lists that include miscellaneous sensations such as hunger, happiness, fatigue, and rhythm.

For the purposes of this chapter, we'll stick with the five senses we learned about in school.

Popular advice recommends that writing include all five senses whenever possible.

Let's evaluate a paragraph that complies with this recommendation:

Patricia heard steps on the front porch, and she smelled sulfur. She could taste bile rising into her throat. She couldn't see anything in the dark, so she groped until she felt the familiar cold metal of her son's baseball bat.

"What's wrong with that?" you might ask. "The paragraph embraces all five senses."

Please review the underlined words. They filter the events through Patricia's perceptions. Let's try a different version:

Someone—or something—stomped across the front porch. The reek of sulfur overwhelmed Patricia's nostrils, and bitter bile burned her throat. She groped in the darkness for a weapon. What was that? Ah, the comforting cold metal of her son's baseball bat.

The second version employs strong verbs that speed readers into the action. Patricia <u>hears</u> stomping, <u>smells</u> sulfur, <u>tastes</u> bitter bile, <u>sees</u> darkness, and <u>feels</u> cold metal.

The words *or something*, set off by em dashes, add to the tension. *The reek of sulfur* leaves no doubt that the odor is unpleasant. *Bitter bile* burns her throat—a more effective taste reference. *Familiar cold metal* changes to *comforting cold metal*, a *tell* that adds to the paragraph.

All filter words (*heard, smelled, taste, see, felt*) are traded for active replacements.

If you don't know what filter words are, you can't avoid them.

Let's review a partial list of filters and their close relatives. I tried to classify them logically, although some words could appear in multiple groups.

<u>See</u>: appear like, become aware of, detect, discern, distinguish, give the impression of, identify, look, look like, note, notice, observe, perceive, realize, recognize, reveal, seem, sense, sight, spot, watch

<u>Smell</u>: detect the smell of, diagnose, get a whiff of, scent, smell like, whiff

<u>Hear</u>: catch, eavesdrop, overhear, listen to, sound, sound like

<u>Touch</u>: feel, feel like

<u>Taste</u>: appreciate, delight in, enjoy, like, relish, savor, take pleasure in

<u>Know</u>: ascertain, assume, believe, bring to mind, cotton on to, decide, deem, discover, figure, gather, get, glean, guess, infer, intuit, learn, posit, regard, remember, suspect, think, understand, wonder

<u>Experience</u>: be subjected to, face, go through, live through, suffer, take in, undergo

<u>Be able to</u>: be capable of, be equal to, be up to the task, can, could, have the ability to, have what it takes to

Dialogue to the rescue?

Analyze the following sentence pairs.

Fabrice stared into the water. The creek <u>looked</u> cold.

Fabrice stared into the creek. "Wow, <u>look</u> at that ice. It must be at least three inches thick." She shivered.

Sneaky, but effective, this provides an example of a filter word that doesn't function as a filter. Fabrice describes the ice on the creek, and readers will understand that it's cold. The shiver reinforces her statement.

Arno <u>heard</u> ringing in both ears.

Arno cupped his ears with his hands. "Will this infernal ringing never stop?

In the second sentence, a combination of body language and dialogue *shows* readers what Arno experiences, without using a single filter word.

This was crazy. Royce <u>knew</u> it, but he couldn't stop himself from popping the question.

"Um," Royce whispered, "I <u>know</u> this is crazy, but would you … will you … marry me?"

Another filter word sneaks into dialogue without functioning as a filter.

By the way, saying that a character knows something is discouraged by editors. Of course your POV character will know _____.

If you need to introduce facts, please find a way that doesn't rely on *know* or *knew*.

Another taboo: several paragraphs of internal monologue. Overdoing a character's private thoughts annoys readers.

Double-up = double-bad.

Do I need to explain why the following examples represent abuse of filter words?

Vivienne <u>listened</u> and <u>heard</u> _____.

Orson <u>looked</u> and <u>saw</u> _____.

Alice <u>whiffed</u> and <u>detected</u> the smell of _____.

Frank <u>tasted</u> and <u>relished</u> the flavor of _____.

Mallory <u>touched</u> her lips and <u>felt</u> _____.

Each sentence repeats the same sensory filter—double-slap on the wrist for offenders. I can't administer your punishment, but dissatisfied agents, editors, and readers will.

More examples of filter rescues:

<u>See</u>

The corporal <u>saw</u> a grenade fly by and land in the foxhole.

A grenade flew by the corporal and landed in the foxhole.

Smell

Joe's belches <u>smelled like</u> booze.

The stench of booze accompanied every belch Joe disgorged.

Hear

Kristina <u>heard</u> a loud scream in the darkness.

A loud scream pierced the darkness enveloping Kristina.

Touch

Alva's fingers <u>touched</u> something wet and sticky.

A sticky liquid adhered to Alva's fingers.

Taste

Johanna smiled. The cake <u>tasted</u> moist and delicious.

Every delicious morsel of cake melted in Johanna's mouth.

Know

Quint <u>knew</u> Sandy wanted to go out with him.

Sandy wanted to go out with Quint.

Experience

Emil <u>experienced</u> a huge stress reaction.

Emil's heart pounded like a gavel, and heat radiated to every extremity.

Be able to

Raquel <u>was able to</u> sleep well for the first time in days.

For the first time in days, Raquel slept well.

Are you ready to attempt a few exercises?

Try to edit away the filter words.

A few of the suggested solutions include what some editors would classify as filters, but as I stated at the outset, all words exist for a reason. If you have to hunt through the solutions with a magnifying glass to find the filter words, they'll pass muster with most people—and although you might doubt it at times, editors are people.

Exercise 1

Guido <u>felt</u> a host of humongous spiders skittering up his arm. Then he <u>felt</u> several sharp pains. They were followed by the <u>feeling</u> that he was suspended, swaying, trapped in a giant web. He <u>heard</u> a squeaky noise somewhere behind him, but he <u>was unable to</u> turn his head to <u>discern</u> what it was.

Suggested solution

A host of humongous spiders skittered up Guido's arm and sank their fangs into his skin. After a moment of disorientation, he found himself suspended, swaying, trapped in a giant web. Somewhere behind him a disembodied squeak sent a shiver down his spine, but the sticky trap immobilized his head, preventing him from investigating the source of the noise.

Exercise 2

Looking up, Prisca <u>noticed</u> that she and her cohort were standing in the blind spot between security cameras. <u>Feeling</u> emboldened, she extended a one-fingered salute in the direction of the CEO's office. Then she <u>heard</u> a voice bellow from somewhere to her left, "Prisca, you're fired."

Suggested solution

Prisca ensured that she and her cohort were standing in the blind spot between security cameras. Then, she stuck out her tongue and extended a one-fingered salute in the direction of the CEO's office. A voice bellowed from somewhere to her left, "Prisca, you're fired."

Exercise 3

All Luisa could <u>hear</u> was silence, a silence so complete she could <u>hear</u> her own pulse. She <u>felt</u> nauseated. *Where am I? The last thing I remember was stepping into the elevator.*

Suggested solution

The silence surrounding Luisa was so complete that the ka-thump of her pulse pounded in her ears. A wave of nausea engulfed her. *Where am I? The last thing I remember was stepping into the elevator.*

Exercise 4

The restaurant <u>smelled like</u> garlic, charbroiled steak, and a faint odor that <u>could have been</u> licorice or fennel. Clint <u>felt</u> hungry, but not hungry enough to chance being poisoned again.

Suggested solution

Tantalizing aromas of garlic, charbroiled steak, and a faint suggestion of licorice or fennel beckoned Clint toward the restaurant. However, his hunger wasn't powerful enough for him to chance being poisoned again.

Exercise 5

Sir Edgar <u>decided</u> he would never <u>be able to</u> reveal his love for Princess Edwina. He <u>knew</u> she loved him too, and she would be in danger if their enemies <u>thought</u> they could get to her through him.

Suggested solution

The bitter truth forced itself on Sir Edgar: He must never reveal his love for Princess Edwina. She loved him too, and she would be in danger if their enemies could get to her through him.

Reader Confusion Part I

Why do you write?

Perhaps you have a dream you want to turn into words, a memoir to share, or an intricate fantasy that begs to be unveiled. Maybe you want to write a biography or a creative-nonfiction essay. At the receiving end will be readers who demand clarity. Confuse them, and you lose them. This chapter suggests alternatives for several instances of confusing wording.

Comma fixes rescue many sentences.

Example 1

Ward spotted the woman who entered the station and waved.

Who is waving? The woman? Ward?

Ward spotted the woman who entered the station, and waved.

The comma implies that Ward is the waver. However, one extra word could clarify even further.

Ward spotted the woman who entered the station, and he waved.

No room for misinterpretation now.

Example 2

Before eating the dog scratched his ear.

For a microsecond, readers might think someone is eating the dog.

Before eating, the dog scratched his ear.

No dog-eating entities here.

Example 3

He stumbled into the cave wearing nothing but boots.

Without a comma, the cave is wearing boots. Really?

He stumbled into the cave, wearing nothing but boots.

A single punctuation mark rescues the sentence without increasing word count.

<u>Example 4</u>

The servants delivered meals on metal trays, covered with aluminum foil.

The comma makes the phrase it precedes refer back to the servants. But the trays are covered with aluminum foil—not the servants.

The servants delivered meals on metal trays covered with aluminum foil.

These servants don't need to protect their brains from alien thought transmissions!

<u>Example 5</u>

Kalan clambered past a throng of enemy forces and tore into a band of troopers armed with nothing but a knife.

A band of troopers armed with nothing but a knife? Seems strange they would share a single weapon.

Kalan clambered past a throng of enemy forces and tore into a band of troopers, armed with nothing but a knife.

Now Kalan is carrying the knife. However, another edit would work even better.

Armed with nothing but a knife, Kalan clambered past a throng of enemy forces and tore into a band of troopers.

Since the most important detail is the phrase that describes Kalan's only weapon, moving it to the beginning gives it the emphasis it deserves.

Word-order adjustment often clarifies meaning.

<u>Example 1</u>

Her fingers tightened the second she entered the arena and saw her opponent.

Readers might expect *tightened* to be followed by a direct object. Her fingers tightened a second *what?*

The second she entered the arena and saw her opponent, her fingers tightened.

With *her fingers tightened* at the end of the sentence, there is no expectation of a direct object.

Example 2

His eyes were red from lack of sleep and unfocussed.

Lack of sleep is the cause of the red and unfocussed eyes. Present wording is clunky.

His eyes were unfocussed and red from lack of sleep.

Now we see better alignment: effect followed by cause.

Example 3

She observed scraps of fabric and boots on the floor.

As worded, readers might expect scraps of fabric and scraps of boots on the floor.

She observed boots and scraps of fabric on the floor.

A word shuffle improves the sentence.

Example 4

Brent imagined soaring over the landscape below and bit his lip.

Readers might see Brent as he imagines soaring over the landscape and as he also imagines whatever comes after *and.*

Brent bit his lip and imagined soaring over the landscape below.

Voilà. Two distinct actions that won't be misconstrued.

Example 5

They gawked at the hole in the ground the bomb had created.

Did the bomb create the ground? Of course not.

They gawked at the hole the bomb had created in the ground.

Much better, although in this case the addition of *that* might clarify even further:

They gawked at the hole <u>that</u> the bomb had created in the ground.

That often eliminates confusion.

In many cases, word flow improves with deletion of *that*. However, you'll find instances where it improves a sentence.

Example 1

Now Jordana knew what had happened, she could relax.

Until readers reach the comma, they might misunderstand the sentence, especially if they are reading the work of an author who has a penchant for comma splices.

The sentence might be mistaken as two separate statements:

Now Jordana knew what had happened. She could relax.

Probably not what the author intended.

Now <u>that</u> Jordana knew what had happened, she could relax.

The addition of *that* identifies the words before the comma as a subordinate clause.

Word order combined with word changes also improve clarity.

Example 1

Marla couldn't withdraw, not with all the people gambling she'd fail behind her.

Were the people gambling that Marla would fail behind her? That doesn't make sense.

Marla couldn't withdraw, not in front of all the people gambling she'd fail.

In this sentence, Marla could be facing the people. Not quite the same meaning.

Marla couldn't withdraw, not while leading all the people who were gambling she'd fail.

Now we see Maria leading, with the people behind her.

However, the original sentence could be rescued with the addition of a single word.

Marla couldn't withdraw, not with all the people gambling she'd fail <u>standing</u> behind her.

<u>Example 2</u>

The team played their first-ever preseason game in Baltimore yesterday.

Is this a new team that played their first-ever preseason game in Baltimore, or is it the first time an established team ever played a preseason game in Baltimore?

Yesterday, for the first time ever, the team played <u>a</u> preseason game in Baltimore.

Edits clarify the situation. Note the impact of *a*, which indicates that this is one of multiple preseason games.

A comma should separate independent clauses joined by *and*.

<u>Example</u>

Francine greeted Harold with a sneer and the other two guards didn't even notice her enter.

Readers might expect Francine to greet Harold with a sneer and whatever follows *and*. Each clause can function as a complete sentence:

Francine greeted Harold with a sneer. The other two guards didn't even notice her enter.

Would a comma solve the ambiguity?

Francine greeted Harold with a sneer, and the other two guards didn't even notice her enter.

Better. However, Harold isn't the person sneering. Let's try this:

With a sneer, Francine greeted Harold, and the other two guards didn't even notice her enter.

Words with more than one meaning? Replace them if context is unclear.

<u>Example 1</u>

Darren had a full lower lip and a spare upper lip.

One of the definitions of *spare* is *thin*. However, readers might think Darren has an extra upper lip, especially if this sentence occurs in fantasy or science fiction.

Darren had a full lower lip and a thin upper lip.

Crystal-clear.

<u>Example 2</u>

While inflation is accelerating, the central bank doesn't intend to raise the prime lending rate.

One of the definitions of *while* is *at the same time as*, which is not the intended meaning in this sentence.

Although inflation is accelerating, the central bank doesn't intend to raise the prime lending rate.

Confusion eliminated.

Consider the various definitions of words such as *tears, pretty, hard, fairly,* and *once.* Would another word function better? You'll find more information covering this point in the next chapter.

Concurrent actions should be possible.

Many authors indicate concurrent actions with *-ing* words. However, when those words are applied incorrectly, they can depict physically impossible events.

<u>Example</u>

Wiggling her feet into sneakers and throwing on a sweater, Katia walked out of the room.

Is it possible for Katia to wiggle her feet into sneakers and throw on a sweater at the same time as she walks out of the room? No.

After wiggling her feet into sneakers and throwing on a sweater, Katia bustled out of the room.

Easy fix, including the replacement of *walked* with its stronger cousin *bustled*. However, the –*ing* words could be eliminated:

Katia wiggled her feet into sneakers and threw on a sweater. Then she bustled out of the room.

Search your WIP for *ing*. You might be amazed at how many matches you find. Check them all for clarity.

Scrutinize every sentence, reading it as though you've never seen it before.

Example 1

Breathing out, a foggy mist formed in front of Sasha's face.

The foggy mist is breathing? Impossible.

As Sasha breathed out, a foggy mist formed in front of her face.

Now Sasha is breathing out.

Example 2

Many towns had upended and derelict boats in their harbors.

Did the towns upend the boats? Readers might assume that *upended* will be followed by a direct object. A change in word order would clarify.

Many towns had derelict and upended boats in their harbors.

Derelict is an adjective; therefore, readers will expect the word following *and* to be another adjective.

Example 3

The space corps was composed of young men without romantic entanglements and flight-trained.

Readers might expect the words following *romantic entanglements* to be another object of the prepositional phrase that begins with *without*.

The space corps was composed of young men flight-trained and without romantic entanglements.

More understandable, but I prefer something like:

The space corps was composed of young men who were flight-trained and had no romantic entanglements.

Put your work away and let it rest.

Narrative you deem clear when you first write a piece often seems obscure after you ignore it for a few weeks—especially when you read it out loud. If the wording disquiets you, even for a microsecond, change it.

Are you ready to test your confusion detector?

To help identify some of the following problems, read the exercises out loud. Don't pause unless you encounter a comma, semicolon, or period.

Exercise 1

The dog scampered toward the bone and growled. Licking its paws, it seized the bone in its teeth and wagged its tail. A dog from two doors down raced toward the yard dragging its leash.

Suggested solution

The bulldog scampered toward the bone. He growled. After licking his paws, he seized the bone in his teeth and wagged his tale. A collie from two doors down raced toward the yard, her leash dragging behind her.

Notes: The solution assigns each dog a gender and breed. Since a dog can't lick its paws and seize a bone in its teeth at the same time, the concurrent action is removed. The yard isn't dragging its leash—clarified with the edits.

Exercise 2

Alwyn's suit was made without synthetic materials and tailored. Its trousers had pleated and close-fitting legs. Hearing a knock, he walked across the room and said, "You're early."

Alwyn's tailored suit, made without synthetic materials, had pleated trousers with close-fitting legs. A knock sounded. He strolled across the room, opened the door, and said, "You're early."

Notes: Several repetitions of *and* are reduced to one occurrence by placing *tailored* and *pleated* before the nouns they modify. Impossible concurrent action is gone. A strong verb, *strolled*, provides a better image than *walked.* Since Alwyn needs to open the door before greeting his visitor, that detail is added.

However, is there a reason to describe Alwyn's suit? As written, the paragraph is clunky. If the description doesn't add to the narrative, maybe it should be deleted:

A knock sounded. Alwyn strolled across the room, opened the door, and said, "You're early."

Exercise 3

Reaching for the canister on the top shelf, a cramp developed in Thelma's shoulder. She groaned and massaged it, it still hurt. She threw the canister on the floor with a frown and the canister broke into several pieces.

Suggested solution

As Thelma reached for the canister on the top shelf, a cramp speared into her shoulder. With a groan, she massaged it. It still hurt. Frowning, she threw the canister onto the floor, where it burst into several pieces.

Notes: The cramp doesn't reach for the canister—Thelma does. She can massage a cramp, but she can't groan it. The second sentence is broken into two to avoid a comma splice. The floor can't frown. Two independent clauses in the last sentence are separated by a comma. Strong verbs are introduced with *speared* and *burst.*

Reader Confusion Part II

Question: What is the goal of writing?

Answer: communication.

The message, whether fiction or nonfiction, might be obvious in the writer's mind but as obscure as dirt to someone else.

Is occasional confusion a big deal?

Yes!

Think of it this way: A woman asks her husband to pick up ice cream. He returns with the wrong flavor. She sends him back to the store. He goes, but he wastes time and becomes irritated.

Readers become irritated when forced to reread sentences. Keep them happy from the first word to the last.

This chapter discusses a few common words and phrases that readers might misinterpret.

About: around; approximately; regarding

They all stood about a yard ...

This could begin a sentence that refers to people standing around in a physical yard or standing approximately a yard away from something. Until readers reach the words following the ellipsis, they have no point of reference.

They all stood about in a yard, eyes skyward, waiting for the super moon to appear.

They all stood approximately a yard away from the entrance, waiting for the store to open.

Edits clarify the author's intent before readers have a chance to falter.

Jordan telephoned Wilson about ten ...

Did Jordan telephone Wilson regarding ten _____ or at approximately ten o'clock? Once again, until readers reach the ellipsis, they won't know.

Jordan telephoned Wilson regarding ten files the hacker had left on the mainframe.

Jordan glanced at his watch—almost ten o'clock. He telephoned Wilson.

Specificity = satisfied readers.

As: because; at the same time as, when

As Mr. Wilde left the room, Debra reached for her cell phone.

Did Debra reach for her cell phone at the same time as Mr. Wilde left the room or because he left the room? Details will prevent ambiguity.

When Mr. Wilde left the room, Debra reached for her cell phone.

Still not as clear as it could be. Let's up our game:

Debra grumbled. Mr. Wilde was not *her favorite teacher. And his rule about no cell phones in class was archaic. Wait. Was he leaving? She reached for her phone.*

Debra's motivation and response are apparent now.

Before: beforehand, prior to; in front of

Jareth bowed before Wentworth.

Did Jareth bow prior to Wentworth, or did he bow in front of Wentworth? Easy fix:

Jareth bowed a moment before Wentworth (did).

Jareth faced Wentworth, bowed, and offered his sword in fealty.

The first example depicts Jareth and Wentworth bowing to a third person or to one another, with Jareth's bow preceding Wentworth's by a moment. The second example portrays Jareth bowing in front of (to) Wentworth.

Call: to dub, name; to telephone

Pam called him Friday.

Did Pam name him Friday, as in *Robinson Crusoe*, or did she telephone him on Friday?

Pam called him <u>on</u> Friday.

The addition of a single word clarifies the meaning. Or consider the following:

Pam telephoned him (on) Friday.

Pam named him Friday.

I encounter this type of muddle most often in period pieces.

Fairly: moderately; quite; equitably

Fairly encompasses numerous disparate meanings. Rather than *fairly*, try targeted adverbs. Better yet, avoid adverbs, opting for stronger verbs and adjectives.

Review the following substitution options.

<u>Moderately:</u> a bit, in part, in some measure, modestly, rather, somewhat, to some extent

<u>Quite:</u> extremely, intensely, markedly, particularly, really, tremendously, very

<u>Equitably:</u> evenhandedly, impartially, justly, legitimately, objectively, rightfully, without bias

Go off: explode in anger; leave

James heard Thomas go off.

Did Thomas throw a temper tantrum? Did he leave?

James heard Thomas slam his fist against the wall.

James heard Thomas close the door after he left the room.

Both sentences, although unambiguous, would be stronger if they weren't filtered through James's ears.

James cringed when Thomas slammed his fist against the wall.

Thomas closed the door after he left the room. James grinned.

We could omit all mention of James. However, his body language strengthens the narrative.

Hard: difficult; inflexible, solid, tough; cruel; intense

"It's so hard," Kim said.

Is Kim touching something solid? Is she facing a difficult dilemma?

"This rock is so hard," Kim said. "I'll never be able to break through."

"I've never faced such a difficult problem," Kim said.

Mystery demystified.

Roberto's face was etched with hard lines.

This sentence is passable but not great. Let's choose precise adjectives that turn mediocre descriptions into powerful images:

Roberto's face was etched with cruel lines.

Roberto's face was etched with intense lines.

Roberto's face was etched with threatening lines.

Each of the preceding sentences conveys a different reason for the lines in Roberto's face.

Incredible: astonishing, extraordinary; absurd, implausible, not believable

Hadley's statement to the judge was incredible.

In context, we might expect Hadley's statement to be implausible. However, it could also be an astonishing revelation. Appropriate details would *show* readers which of the two meanings is correct:

Hadley's statement to the judge was so ~~incredible~~ absurd that everyone in the courtroom burst out laughing.

Hadley's statement to the judge revealed an ~~incredible~~ astonishing fact: He was left-handed and couldn't have committed the murder.

I occasionally watch a popular courtroom reality series. One of the judges says *incredible*—a lot—and although I know what she means (not believable), I wince whenever I hear it.

My suggestion: Rely on *non-credible* to indicate something that is absurd, implausible, or not believable.

Pretty: beautiful [adjective]; rather [adverb]

Jason looked at the pretty little girl.

Is the girl rather little, or is she a little girl who is pretty?

Jason gawked at the gorgeous young girl.

Jason gazed at the cute toddler.

Precision eliminates any opportunity for misunderstanding.

Jason arrived in a pretty yellow cape.

Besides the awkwardness of the wording, is the cape quite yellow, or is the yellow cape pretty?

Jason whirled into view, flourishing a banana-yellow cape.

Jason flounced through the door, wearing a yellow cape adorned with sequins.

The edited sentences evoke unambiguous images.

Right: right-hand or starboard direction; directly

Margarita and George turned right into the courtyard.

Did they turn in a right-hand direction, or directly into the courtyard?

Margarita and George turned right, into the courtyard.

The comma tells readers that Margarita and George turned toward the right.

Not the correct interpretation?

Margarita and George turned directly into the courtyard.

The edit leaves no uncertainty.

Secrete: to excrete; to hide

The giant monster secreted the stuff.

Although context might provide clarity, why not rely on words that won't create confusion?

The giant monster excreted slimy mucus wherever it crawled.

The giant monster stole shiny baubles from nearby villages, scuttled into the forest, and hid its treasures in a cave.

Secretion or secrecy? Edits remove ambiguity.

Start: to flinch, jerk, jump; to begin

If Lorene started, the rope would break. She held her breath.

Unless the author has included appropriate details, readers might stall at this point.

If Lorene flinched, the frayed rope would break. She held her breath.

If Lorene stepped forward (began), the rope would break. She held her breath.

Edited versions explain the circumstances.

Tears: rips, slits [verb]; rips, slits [noun]; moisture produced by crying [noun]

Larry couldn't control the tears.

If *tears* refers to crying, we must ensure that the circumstances are clear; otherwise this could refer to rips in clothing or maybe gashes in the panels of a hot-air balloon:

The tears came on suddenly.

Sorry, folks, these tears could still refer to crying or to rips. Let's offer more details and perhaps segue into a couple of story ideas:

Larry tried to hold his emotions in check, but he couldn't control the tears that rolled down his cheeks and into the ropes binding his chest.

Larry attempted to mend the tears in the sail, but the wind whipped it out of his hands.

No puzzled frowns from readers here.

This: so, to an indicated degree or extent [adverb]; referring to a nearby thing or situation [adjective]; an event, a person, or something that has just been mentioned [pronoun]

Alexis had never felt this ...

Until readers reach the words following the ellipsis, *this* could be interpreted as an adverb, an adjective, or a pronoun.

Alexis had never felt ~~this~~ so embarrassed.

Alexis had never felt ~~this~~ such a sensation.

Alexis had never felt ~~this~~ love before.

Replacing *this* with the underlined words produces concise sentences.

While: although, even though, whereas; during the time; at the same time as (when, meanwhile)

While Nicole grasped the steering wheel with a white-knuckled grip ...

Readers must absorb ten words before they can begin to understand what comes next.

Although Nicole grasped the steering wheel with a white-knuckled grip, the car spun out of control.

Nicole grasped the steering wheel with a white-knuckled grip. Meanwhile, Sharon dialed 911.

No risk of misinterpretation.

While some of the new hires worked diligently, others just gossiped and laughed.

Did some of the new hires work diligently even though others gossiped and laughed, or at the same time as others gossiped and laughed?

During coffee break, some of the new hires worked diligently. Others just gossiped and laughed.

Adding a specific time, *during coffee break*, helps clarify the sentence.

Wind: to enfold, wrap (around) [verb]; to meander, snake, zigzag [verb]; to tighten (as a spring) [verb]; an air current [noun]

Not only does *wind* cause problems in present tense, but also in past tense:

An invisible force wound around Janice's legs.

This sentence is vague as written. Envision legs immobilized by invisible bonds:

An invisible force wrapped around Janice's legs.

Or imagine the force traveling around her legs.

An invisible force zigzagged around Janice's legs.

Sometimes *wound* is misinterpreted as a physical injury. Although it's unlikely that people would confuse the verb *wind* with the noun *wind* and likewise with *wound*, it can (and does) happen.

What can we learn from these examples?

An important lesson: Let your writing rest before final edits. Then, read each paragraph in isolation, once silently and again out loud, to identify areas that might confuse or distract readers.

Stacked Modifiers

This chapter is a primer on stacked modifiers—multiple words that describe a noun.

Guideline 1: Adjectives follow a specific sequence.

Our brains act as automatic sorters with two or three descriptors, organizing word-strings without conscious thought. However, we may fumble when we encounter lengthy phrases.

<u>Quantity comes before color.</u>

Would you ever say *I bought ~~white two~~ dresses*? No. You understand that the correct phrasing is *I bought two white dresses*.

<u>Opinion precedes size, which precedes physical quality.</u>

The ~~muscular, small, horrible~~ *man made an obscene gesture.*

The horrible, small, muscular man made an obscene gesture.

<u>Age precedes nationality.</u>

The ~~American elderly~~ *woman brandished an anti-abortion sign.*

The elderly American woman brandished an anti-abortion sign.

<u>Material precedes purpose.</u>

The ~~sports nylon~~ *leggings chafed my legs.*

The nylon sports leggings chafed my legs.

The generally accepted order is:

<u>Quantity</u> (fifteen, a few, several, many, heaps of, scads)

<u>Opinion</u> (fantastic, horrible, good, bad, beautiful, funny)

<u>Size</u> (big, small, gigantic, queen-sized, bite-sized, petite)

<u>Physical quality</u> (overweight, muscular, emaciated, robust)

<u>Age</u> (elderly, teenage, retired, newborn, adolescent)

<u>Shape</u> (oval, triangular, asymmetrical, octagonal, irregular)

<u>Color</u> (white, black, red, checkered, multicolor, piebald)

<u>Nationality or place of origin</u> (American, Chinese, Californian)

<u>Material</u> (paper, fur, glass, flour, nylon, metal, cardboard)

<u>Purpose</u> (sports, sparring, refrigerating, culinary, safety)

Guideline 2: Limit the number of stacked modifiers.

This is a logical derivative of the previous section.

Read these sentences out loud:

Several disgusting, tiny, skinny, oval black bugs marched across the carpet.

Three tall, robust, retired American men patrolled the neighborhood every night.

A dozen delicious, bite-sized, day-old chocolate doughnuts lay on the shelf, tempting me to break my diet.

Did you get lost in the word parades? The payoff for repetition is not emphasis, but confusion, and the abundance of commas results in choppy reading.

Try to limit the total adjectives and adverbs in any given group to three or fewer.

Let's revisit the preceding sentences:

<u>Sentence 1</u>

<u>*Several disgusting, tiny, skinny, oval black*</u> *bugs marched across the carpet.*

Do we need both *tiny* and *skinny?* Is *oval* necessary? Readers will have a preconceived notion of what bugs look like. We can probably drop *disgusting* as well, because opinion adjectives break POV if not reported through the correct character. Furthermore, most readers will have their own feelings about bugs.

<u>*Several skinny black*</u> *bugs marched across the carpet.*

This sentence is easier to read. Did it lose anything with the edits? Note that *several* modifies *skinny black bugs*; therefore, commas are unnecessary. [See Guideline 4.]

Sentence 2

Three tall, robust, retired American men patrolled the neighborhood every night.

Tall and *robust*, although they embrace different connotations, could be distilled to one word. Is it necessary to describe the men as *American?* Unless the reference is crucial to the story, we could drop it.

Three robust, retired men patrolled the neighborhood every night.

Essential details have been preserved. As per Guideline 4, some editors would be happy to omit the comma.

If nationality is important, *men* could be changed to *Americans*, and gender could be clarified via context.

Sentence 3

A dozen delicious, bite-sized, day-old chocolate doughnuts lay on the shelf, tempting me to break my diet.

Delicious is an opinion word. Since the doughnuts tempt the protagonist, their tastiness is implied. *Bite-sized* is an unimportant detail.

A dozen day-old chocolate doughnuts lay on the shelf, tempting me to break my diet.

Is your mouth watering yet? Day-old doughnuts? Maybe not.

Guideline 3: Hyphenate connected modifiers when they precede nouns, but not when they follow.

The *high-definition* television teetered on top of the trash.

The television teetering on top of the trash was *high definition*.

Her *over-the-top* theatrical performance disgusted the audience.

Her theatrical performance was *over the top*, disgusting the audience.

Hyphens inform human eyes that the connected words form a single idea.

Note the lack of hyphens in modifiers following nouns; although to avoid confusion, hyphenation might be warranted for the given examples. This leads to the next point.

Exception: If misinterpretation is likely or possible with modifiers following nouns, connect the words with hyphens:

Steven King is <u>well known</u> for his horror novels.

Without a hyphen, readers might for a microsecond assume that *well* refers to Steven King's health. Some sources recommend that all instances of *well* + [modifier] phrases be connected by hyphens.

A better version would be:

Steven King is <u>well-known</u> for his horror novels.

Another example:

Ted is <u>dead serious</u>.

To avoid making readers think for a moment that Ted is dead, a hyphen is recommended.

Ted is <u>dead-serious</u>.

A third example:

Marie is <u>high spirited</u>.

Is Marie high on drugs, or is she *high-spirited*?

Easier to understand:

Marie is <u>high-spirited</u>.

Read just the first word whenever you encounter stacked modifiers following a noun. Could your writing be misinterpreted? If yes, hyphenate.

Another exception: Guideline 3 doesn't apply to *very* and adverbs ending in *ly*.

The *very old* man gulped down his coffee.

The *sparsely applied SPF-60* sunblock didn't protect Jerold in the areas he missed.

Careful with *-ly* words.

The *lovely-looking* sky clouded over.

Although *lovely* ends in *ly*, it's an adjective, not an adverb; therefore, a hyphen is suggested.

To locate more examples and guidelines for hyphenated adjectives, search the internet for *adjectives hyphenated before but not after a noun Chicago Manual of Style*.

Guideline 4: A comma isn't required after a descriptor that modifies an adjective-noun combination.

The *grumpy old man* mumbled as he walked.

Grumpy describes *old man*.

The men unloaded *twenty high-definition TVs* from the truck.

Twenty describes *high-definition TVs*.

His *tight blue T-shirt* clung to his body.

Tight describes *blue T-shirt*.

Hyphenated modifiers:

Here's a partial list of compound modifiers that could retain their hyphenation when they follow a noun. Apply your best judgment in order to create clear phrasing and maintain a consistent approach.

A
Absent-minded

B
Best-known, bite-sized, black-and-blue, black-and-white, broken-hearted

C
Cholesterol-free, class-action

D
Day-old, dead-serious, dead-to-rights, deep-rooted, double-breasted

E
Ear-piercing, English-speaking, eye-popping

F
Fast-moving, fat-free, first-hand, first-rate, full-length, full-scale

G
Good-looking, good-natured

H
Hand-to-hand, hand-to-mouth, heart-rending, high-minded, high-risk, high-spirited

I
Ice-cold, ill-advised, ill-at-ease, ill-humored

K
Kind-hearted

L
Last-minute, long-lasting, long-winded, low-key, low-risk

M
Mean-spirited, meat-eating, middle-aged

N
Narrow-minded, never-ending

O
Off-limits, old-fashioned, open-minded, over-the-top

P
Part-time, paycheck-to-paycheck

Q
Queen-sized, quick-witted

R
Ready-to-eat, record-breaking, red-blooded, red-handed

S
Second-hand, short-haired, skin-deep, slow-moving, small-town, state-of-the-art, strong-willed, sugar-free, sure-footed

T
Thought-provoking, tight-fisted, time-saving, tone-deaf, top-notch

U
Up-to-date, up-to-the-minute

W
Waist-high, well-known, well-made, well-paid, well-thought-of, well-written, wide-eyed, world-famous, world-renown

Test your understanding.

Which of the following sentences are incorrect?

1. The British absent minded professor spoke in a monotone.

2. The British professor was absent minded and spoke in a monotone.

3. The metal octagonal disk glinted in the sun.

4. The children ate several oatmeal gigantic cookies.

5. The couple celebrated with a huge fantastic party.

6. Bill's ear piercing scream could be heard three rooms away.

7. The dappled overweight horse clip-clopped down the street.

8. Harry's diet consisted of cholesterol free, sugar free foods.

9. A cloudless, blue sky stretched from horizon to horizon.

10. My big red horrible running shoes chafed my heels.

ANSWER: Every sentence contains at least one mistake. Review the corrected versions below.

1. The absent-minded British professor spoke in a monotone. [See Guideline 1, Guideline 3.]

2. The British professor was absent-minded and spoke in a monotone. [See Guideline 3 exceptions.]

3. The octagonal metal disk glinted in the sun. [See Guideline 1.]

4. The children ate several gigantic oatmeal cookies. [See Guideline 1, Guideline 4.]

5. The couple celebrated with a fantastic huge party. [See Guideline 1, Guideline 4. A comma after *fantastic* might please some readers.]

6. Bill's ear-piercing scream could be heard three rooms away. [See Guideline 3.]

7. The overweight dappled horse clip-clopped down the street. [See Guideline 1, Guideline 4.]

8. Harry's diet consisted of cholesterol-free, sugar-free foods. [See Guideline 3.]

9. A cloudless blue sky stretched from horizon to horizon. [See Guideline 4.]

10. My horrible, big red running shoes chafed my heels. [See Guideline 1, Guideline 4. You might feel happier with a comma after *big*.]

Typos and Errors

If you're like me, you don't look forward to proofreading.

It's time-consuming; you're trapped while you go over words you've already read multiple times; you feel as though your creativity is in stasis until you're finished.

But smart authors have learned techniques to streamline the task.

Before we begin, do you know the difference between editing and proofreading?

Proofreading is the final step after you've made your editorial revisions. It's the stage where you detect and correct errors in punctuation, spelling, and grammar. Ideally, you should complete all other modifications first.

You can shorten the proofreading phase by using spell-check and grammar-check while you write. You'll identify many mistakes as they occur. If you haven't already done so, fine-tune your word processor's proofing settings. Do you want to check for fragments and run-on sentences? Passive sentences? Do you prefer to ignore words containing numbers? Set the options before you compose your first line.

Some authors don't worry about mistakes during the initial draft. However, I've found that early errors sometimes escape undetected, only to flash their ugly faces after a book has been published.

Begin with the basics.

Allocate specific time for proofreading, and anticipate potential interruptions. Put away your smartphone, turn off the radio and television, forget social media, and ignore your email.

Rather than proofread an entire book during a weekend, dedicate smaller sessions over several days. Your mind will be fresher, and you'll be more likely to notice mistakes. Pause once every hour to do something like walk the dog, spend two minutes on the treadmill, eat a snack, or go outside for some fresh air.

Make a copy of your document so you can refer to it if necessary. Back up frequently as you work. This allows you to recover from blunders like erroneous search-and-replace operations or unintended deletions. I keep several backups, naming them *StoryName001*, *StoryName002*, *StoryName003*, etc. as I revise.

Scientific research reveals that a moderate level of noise, about seventy decibels, stimulates concentration and creativity. This is comparable to what you'd hear in a busy coffee shop. Capitalizing on this research, sites like Coffitivity.com provide streaming audio you can listen to while you work.

Increase the zoom of your word processing software to about 120 percent. If you need to move your head from side to side while you read a line, the percentage is too high. Try different settings until you find one that works for you.

Perform a separate review for errors such as omitted punctuation marks at the ends of sentences, missing closing quotes or parentheses, and formatting errors that force words onto new lines. This review is easier if you activate your word processor's option to reveal paragraph marks and other hidden formatting symbols.

Some authors copy and paste their work into a new document. Then they switch to a different, larger typeface and/or change the font color. However, I prefer the percentage method in the previous tip. It doesn't alter the formatting of your novel, which means you don't have to change anything after you complete the proofing process. Edits are made in the main document, saving time and aggravation.

An alternate approach is to change the font face in your main document with each proofing pass, restoring it to your font of choice before publication. This often helps pinpoint quotation marks that face the wrong way, and other irregularities that might otherwise be missed.

Refer to a dictionary, thesaurus, or grammar textbook if you're unsure of anything.

Based on your previous slipups, create a list of common mistakes, and correct them in a separate proofing step.

Partway through, if you discover a new type of error you've made several times, bookmark your current spot with something like *zzzzz* or *qqqqq*. Search for occurrences of the error and correct them. Then, you can return to your bookmark and continue where you left off. I use *zzzzz* whenever I want to remember my current position, whether it's during the first draft, editorial review, or proofreading process.

Proof your work at least twice: once for accuracy of facts, and again for spelling, grammar, and punctuation mistakes.

Homonyms confuse many authors. Should it be *here* or *hear? peek, peak,* or *pique? peel* or *peal?* Don't guess.

Apostrophes never form plurals. The plural of *computer* is *computers*. If you're talking about several Volkswagens, the correct plural of the abbreviated form is *VWs* not *VW's*.

Apostrophes form contractions. Use them correctly. Should it be *your* or *you're? Their* or *they're?* And the big one so many writers get wrong: *its* or *it's?*

Apostrophes also indicate possession. If several people own an object, the apostrophe follows the *s: The Barkers' car went to the shop for repair.* If one person owns it, the apostrophe usually precedes the *s: Mr. Barker's car went to the shop for repair.*

Watch for comma splices.

Check for spaces between the last word in a sentence and its closing punctuation.

Things named after people or places generally begin with capitals. Therefore, *caesarian section* is incorrect. It should be *Caesarian section.* Our planet is *Earth*, but dirt is *earth.*

Check for consistency. Do you use *goodbye* in one place but *good-bye* in another?

Some authors set aside a session to proofread their writing backwards. They say this helps discover errors they would otherwise overlook, such as missing words the brain tries to fill in when they read from left to right.

Assess all numbers for misplaced decimal points, commas, and numerical descriptors. Is the world's population 6,974 million, or is it 6.974 billion?

Verify links in e-books, including internet sites and internal document bookmarks.

If you decide to make an editorial change to a paragraph, read the previous two paragraphs and the following two to ensure you haven't introduced unnecessary repetition or a break in flow. You should follow any such changes by an additional proofreading session of the entire document.

Check for consistency in formatting. You should configure the same font size and weight for all comparable sections.

If you discover a formatting problem you can't eliminate, copy and paste the offending passage into a text file. Delete the words from your main document, copy them from your text file back into their original location, and reformat if required.

Print out your WIP.

Some errors will be more obvious on printed copies of your work than on your computer screen. The more methods you use to review what you've written, the more mistakes you'll catch.

Use a colored highlighter to mark necessary changes. Highlight every punctuation mark with a second color. Should you have used a question mark instead of a period? Have you typed two exclamation points? Do you *need* an exclamation point? Have you closed all quotes and parentheses?

Mistakes in long words are conspicuous. Pay attention to short words. They're easy to misuse or omit.

Always proofread your front matter and sections such as *About the Author*. This includes ISBN, title, table of contents, and your name. (Yes, authors have been known to misspell their own names.)

Review every chapter heading and title. An error in large, bold type will alienate readers.

Put your writing away for a few days and then reevaluate it with fresh eyes.

Ask someone else to read your printed copy. The person you choose should have an excellent command of grammar and spelling. Your proofreader might also find plot holes and inconsistencies you missed during your editorial review.

Harness the power of audio.

Your ears often catch what your eyes miss. Many anomalies are more obvious to the brain when heard rather than seen. This includes missing commas and similarly spelled words such as *desert* and *dessert*.

Try these audio-related tips:

Read out loud, *slowly*. Speak every word. During a fast read, your brain will attempt to smooth out mistakes.

Ask someone else to read your work to you.

Dictate your writing into an audio file on your computer and then play it back.

Use the text-to-speech capabilities of Word or your PC. This option can save you from laryngitis if you're proofing a long novel. Even if you whisper, your throat may protest from overuse.

For PC users: If you click the *Start* button and search for *Change-text-to-speech settings*, you can slow down the voice for the following two tips.

1. Word provides a *Speak selected text* option that allows your computer to read portions of text out loud. Microsoft publishes full details at:

http://office.microsoft.com/en-001/word-help/using-the-speak-text-to-speech-feature-HA102066711.aspx

2. Save your document as a PDF file, then click on *View ==> Read Out Loud ==> Activate Read Out Loud*. Select *Read Out Loud* a second time and choose one of the following options:

- *Deactivate Read Out Loud*
- *Read This Page Only*
- *Read to End of Document*

If you don't like the voice(s) on your PC or Mac, explore the web for third-party software. Search for *free text-to-speech voices*.

Explore a free online service like Yakitome.com. Yakitome allows you to copy and paste text, or upload an entire document. The site will even create an audio file for download to your computer.

Exploit your e-reader.

Read your document on an e-reader, following each word with your finger. Highlight mistakes or areas you need to fix.

Try text-to-speech if your e-reader supports it. Not sure? Look for speakers and a headphone jack on your device, or go to its online product information page to find complete specs.

Word Bloat

One definition for *bloat:* to puff up, to make vain or conceited.

Do you want your work to puff up with unnecessary words? To seem vain or conceited?

This chapter provides more than 250 phrases you can delete or replace with shorter alternatives.

Let's analyze a few examples.

Example 1

Hayden didn't pay any attention to the pain in his shoulder as he took a seat in the restaurant booth and had a quick look at his watch. I have time to spare, he thought.

Do you see any areas where you could cut words?

Hayden ignored the pain in his shoulder as he sank into the restaurant booth and peeked at his watch. I'm early, he thought.

The edits save a dozen words and move the narrative at a quicker pace.

Example 2

Bella accessed the street by means of the alley. In short order she'd meet her cheating fiancé head-on. He'd deny it, of course, in spite of the fact that she had read all of the text messages. Was she ready and willing to forgive him?

Did you spot the redundancies?

Bella accessed the street via the alley. Soon she'd confront her cheating fiancé. He'd deny it, of course, although she had read all the text messages. Was she prepared to forgive him?

More than a dozen words saved, although in this situation some of the redundancies might be appropriate for Bella's thoughts.

Example 3

Pol was ready and willing to join the club, but time and time again the membership committee had, for all intents and purposes, told him they would never give his application the go-ahead.

You should be getting good at this by now.

Pol was eager to join the club, but the membership committee had repeatedly implied that they would never approve his application.

Note the different interpretation of *ready and willing—eager* in this case versus *prepared* in Example 2—an excellent reason for avoiding the phrase.

Recognize frequent offenders.

Your suspicious nature should activate whenever you encounter phrases that begin with *cause, for, give, go, have, in, make, not,* or *take:*

Cause

Cause concern: concern, upset, worry

Cause confusion: baffle, confuse, perplex

Cause pain: distress, hurt, wound

Cause surprise: alarm, shock, surprise

For

For all intents and purposes: [delete]

For the most part: [delete]

For the purpose of: to

For the time being: meantime, meanwhile

Give

Give a heads-up: alert, caution, forewarn

Give a nod: agree, concur, nod

Give a nod to: approve, endorse, support

Give a sigh: sigh

Give a salute: acknowledge, greet, salute

Give a thumbs-up: approve, endorse, support

Give a wink: wink

Give chase: chase, pursue, track

Give the go-ahead: approve, authorize, consent

Go

Go along with: accept, agree, concur

Go back over: rethink, retrace, review

Go by car: drive

Go by plane: fly

Go on foot: walk

Go through: endure; read; use

Go walking: stride, stroll, walk

Have

Have a nap: doze, nap, snooze

Have a tendency: favor, incline, tend

Have a discussion: consider, debate, discuss

Have a conversation: chat, converse, discuss

Have an idea: conceive, imagine, visualize

Have a quick look: glance, look, peek

Have to: must, should

In

In a good mood: cheerful, happy, jovial

In a little while: forthwith, soon, straightaway

In actual fact: [delete]

In good health: fit, hale, healthy

In regard(s) to: apropos, concerning, regarding

In the event that: if

In the near future: directly, momentarily, pronto, shortly, soon

In the process of: [delete]

In short order: pronto, quickly, soon

In spite of the fact that: although, nevertheless, still

In terms of: [delete]

Make

Make a decision: choose, decide, resolve

Make a move: move, rouse, stir

Make an announcement: announce, declare, proclaim

Make it to: arrive, reach

Not

Not have much confidence: distrust, doubt, suspect

Not honest: deceitful, dishonest, misleading

Not important: inconsequential, insignificant, unimportant

Not on time: late, overdue, tardy

Not pay attention: disregard, ignore, snub

Not remember: forget

Take

Take a seat: park, settle, sit

Take an enormous toll: distress, torment, torture

Take captive: capture, catch, ensnare

Take care of: handle, manage, undertake

Take exception: disapprove, object, protest

Take into account: allow, consider, include

Take notice: detect, notice, see

More redundancies:

Again and again: constantly, repeatedly, repetitively

Against the law: illegal, illicit, unlawful

Are reflective of: echo, mirror, reflect

As a matter of fact: actually, really

As opposed to: versus

As to whether: whether

At all times: always

At the present time: currently, now, today

At the end of the day: eventually, finally, ultimately

Be aware of: discern, know, recognize

Be in love with: adore, love, worship

Be watchful: guard, observe, watch

By means of: per [dated], through, via

By virtue of the fact that: because, since

Cease and desist: cease, desist, discontinue, stop

Continue on in perpetuity: endure, last forever

Cut down on: lessen, lower, reduce

Decrease in strength: abate, dilute, weaken

Do away with: abolish, eliminate, kill

Due to the fact that: because, since

Figure out: decipher, realize, solve

Filled to capacity: brimming, full, packed

Get out of: escape, exit, leave

Given the fact that: since

Go around and around in circles: circle, rehash reoccur

Go to play golf: golf

Going to: will

Inasmuch as: because, since, whereas

Increase in strength: increase, intensify, strengthen

Intend to: will

It is important to note that: [delete]

Lack the ability to: cannot

Lead to the destruction of: destroy

Meet head-on: challenge, confront, tackle

More so than ever before: especially, more than ever, particularly

Need to: must

Needless to say: [delete]

Null and void: invalid, void, worthless

Offer a suggestion: propose, recommend, suggest

On a regular basis: consistently, often, regularly

Pick out: choose, pick, select

Pick up on: detect, notice, see

Play up: accentuate, emphasize, stress

Put together: assemble, build, construct

Put off: delay, postpone, stall

Ready and willing: eager; prepared, ready

Result in a decrease: decrease, dwindle, shrink

Result in an increase: expand, increase, multiply

Seeing as how: because, since

Spell out: clarify, detail, explain

Spot on: appropriate, correct, precise

There were times when they: every time they, whenever they

Time and time again: often, recurrently, repeatedly

To the point: concise, succinct, terse

Tried and true: established, tested, verified

Utter an objection: challenge, object, protest

Well-thought-of: reputable, respectable, trustworthy

With reference to: apropos, concerning, regarding

With time to spare: early

Occasional redundancies add personality to writing.

To prevent repetition or awkward wording, redundancies sometimes provide viable alternatives.

Readers expect dialogue to include clichés and *occasional* superfluous words. Exploit every possible tool to differentiate characters' voices and make them believable.

Tag, you're it.

Locate and remove redundancies in the following:

Exercise 1

Sadie gave a wink to her neighbor and made a decision to ask him out on a date. "Hi," she said. "Would you like to have coffee with me?"

He didn't pay any attention to her but went walking by as though he hadn't heard.

She gave a sigh. *Must be out of phase again.*

Suggested solution

Sadie winked at her neighbor. "Hi. Would you like to have coffee with me?"

He ignored her, walking by as though he hadn't heard.

She sighed. *Must be out of phase again.*

Notes: Besides the obvious redundancies, we know Sadie is talking; therefore, a dialogue tag is unnecessary in the first paragraph. Her dialogue *shows* she's asking her neighbor out on a date, so there's no need to state the obvious.

Exercise 2

Steve went by car on a regular basis to the golf course. He went to play golf twice every week and usually wasn't on time, because he wouldn't remember his clubs until he made it to the next block. Then in actual fact he'd have to turn around.

<u>Suggested solution</u>

Steve drove often to the golf course. He hit the greens twice weekly and was usually late, because he'd forget his clubs until he reached the next block. Then he'd have to turn around.

Notes: Redundancies have been removed. However, an idiom, *hit the greens*, was added to eliminate the repetition of *golf.* Steve seems distracted. That distraction could form the basis of a comedic or mysterious plot.

Master Table of Contents

This table of contents encompasses both volumes of *The Writer's Lexicon*. Page numbers are based on the print editions. You can download a PDF version of this ToC at:

https://kathysteinemann.com/toc.pdf

Afterword

The English language contains more than one million words, and new ones are created every day. In these pages I've focused on the most common repetitions and problems encountered by writers.

Did I miss something you'd like to see included in a third volume?

Please get in touch:

Author@KathySteinemann.com

P.S. If you like this book, please leave a review.

Thanks!

Kathy

About the Author

Kathy Steinemann, Grandma Birdie to her grandkids, is an award-winning author. She has loved words for as long as she can remember, especially when the words are frightening or futuristic or funny.

Her career has taken varying directions, including positions as editor of a small-town paper, computer-network administrator, and webmaster. She has also worked on projects in commercial art and cartooning.

Kathy's Website

KathySteinemann.com

Books by Kathy Steinemann

Humor
- *Nag Nag Nag: Megan and Emmett Volume I*
- *Rule 1: Megan and Emmett Volume II*

Speculative Fiction
- *Envision: Future Fiction*

Multiple Genre
- *Suppose: Drabbles, Flash Fiction, and Short Stories*

Alternative History
- *Vanguard of Hope: Sapphire Brigade Book 1*
- *The Doctor's Deceit: Sapphire Brigade Book 2*

Nonfiction
- *The Writer's Lexicon*
- *The Writer's Lexicon Volume II*
- *CreateSpace Graphics Primer*
- *IBS-IBD Fiber Charts*
- *The IBS Compass*
- *Practical and Effective Tips for Learning Foreign Languages*
- *Top Tips for Packing Your Suitcase*
- *Top Tips for Travel by Air*

Multilingual
- *Life, Death and Consequences*
- *Leben, Tod und Konsequenzen (German Edition)*
- *Matthew and the Pesky Ants*
- *Matthias und die verflixten Ameisen (German Edition)*

Made in the USA
San Bernardino, CA
03 June 2020